The New Children's Bible

Anne de Vries

CF4·K

ISBN 978-1-85792-838-9

This edition published in 2004 by
Christian Focus Publications Ltd,
Geanies House, Tain, Ross-shire,
IV20 1TW, Scotland, UK.
www.christianfocus.com

Cover illustration and inside illustrations by Fred Apps
Printed in Malta

This book was presented to

......The children of Montem School......

on
......17th July, 2020......

by
......Mrs David ☺......

With love and special memories
from my 22 years at the
school xx

Contents

THE OLD TESTAMENT

THE NEW TESTAMENT

The Old
Testament

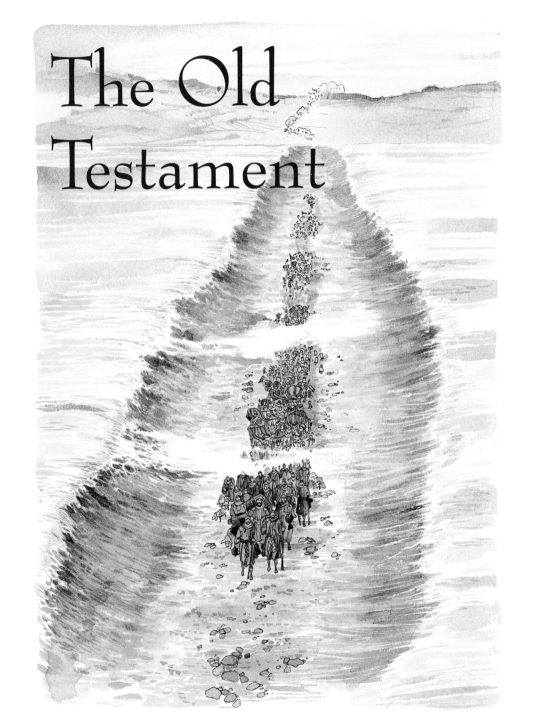

Why the week has seven days

Read: Genesis 1

In the beginning God made heaven and earth. In heaven everything was beautiful, bright and happy. God lived there with the angels but nobody lived on the earth. It was formless and empty and dark. Then God thought he would make the earth a place where plants and animals could live. He said, 'Let there be light,' and light appeared because everything that God commands happens.

When evening came, it grew dark again and God said, 'Let us call the light, day, and the dark, night.' That was how the first day was born and how it ended. On the second day, God went on with his work to make the world. He said, 'Now let there be a blue sky above the earth!' No sooner had he commanded it than the sky was there.

On the third day, God made some dry places. He said, 'The water will be called the sea, and the dry parts, land.' After that God made all kinds of plants to grow. He made flowers and trees and grass and wheat.

On the fourth day, God made the sun. Early in the morning the sun lay low in the sky, but as the day passed it climbed higher in the sky and gave off soft warm light. Then, as evening came, the sun dropped lower and lower until finally it disappeared from sight. That night, however, it didn't get quite so dark, for God had made the moon and twinkling stars. God said, 'From now on the sun will shine in the daytime and the moon will shine at night.'

On the fifth day God made the fish in the sea and the birds in the air. He made big fish and little fish. He made them graceful, and their scales shone with many colours under the water. God gave the birds magnificent feathers with all the colours of the rainbow and He gave them voices so that they could sing as they flew among the trees. He taught the birds how to build their nests where they would lay their eggs from which baby birds would come.

The sixth day was wonderful. First, God made all the animals, like horses, cows, rabbits and sheep. He made cats, dogs, elephants and mice - all the living things, both male and female. Then God said, 'Let us make man.' So God made the first man and called him Adam. God said, 'Adam, you will look after all the things I have made. You will rule over the fish, the birds and all the animals. All of them must obey you but you must obey me!' Adam listened carefully and understood.

The sixth day came and passed and on the seventh day God rested from his work, for in six days he had made everything. But there was one tree from which Adam was not allowed to eat. That tree stood in the middle of the garden and it was called the tree of the knowledge of good and evil.

Adam and Eve

Read: Genesis 2

God took good care of Adam. He made a lovely garden for him to live in, where flowers bloomed and birds sang. The garden was a wonderful place where Adam could be happy for ever. It was called the Garden of Eden. Sometimes God would come and talk to Adam when he was walking in the garden. When Adam heard God's voice he was happy to have God so close to him. Adam took care of the garden and ate as much as he pleased of the things that grew there.

God had told Adam: 'You may eat from any of the trees, but not from this one. If you eat the fruit from this tree you will die!' Adam listened carefully to God's instructions and did not eat the fruit.

One day God brought all the animals to Adam. He asked Adam to give each of them a name. But God also knew that Adam needed a friend. So after Adam had named all the animals God put Adam to sleep and when he woke there was a woman with him. God had made her for him, to be his wife and friend. Her name was Eve. Adam took Eve with him and showed her everything in the garden. They were both very happy. They had no pain or sickness. They were never sad or afraid for they lived close to God. God was their Father and they were his children.

The Snake, the Fruit and Sin

Read: Genesis 3

One day Eve was walking in the garden when she found herself close to the forbidden tree. As she approached it she heard a voice. It wasn't Adam and it certainly wasn't God. Eve looked and saw that it was a snake speaking to her. It stared at her with small beady eyes and said: 'Listen to me, is it true that you may not eat of any tree in the garden?' Eve answered, 'We may eat of all the trees, except this one. God told us that if we eat the fruit of this tree, we shall die.'

Then the sly snake whispered, 'Did God really say that? If you eat the fruit from this tree you will be happier than you are now, and you will be as wise and strong as God Himself!'

Eve looked at the fruit. It was beautiful, surely it must taste delicious too. Besides, Eve wanted to be as wise as God! Eve reached up and picked one. Part of the fruit she gave to Adam and part she kept for herself. God had clearly warned them not to eat the fruit from this tree, but they ate anyway. They had disobeyed God. No sooner had they taken the first bite than they knew that the snake had lied. They could feel it in their hearts, for they were no longer happy. They felt afraid, sad, and ashamed, because for the first time they noticed they had no clothes. Quickly they picked large leaves to cover themselves. Then they heard the voice of God! The voice, which had always made them happy before, made them terribly afraid and they ran to hide in the bushes.

They hoped that God would not find them. God knows everything so of course he found them. He called to Adam, 'Adam, where are you?' Adam and Eve trembled as they came out from behind the bushes. They were so ashamed that they didn't dare to look at God. 'Did you eat the fruit from that tree?' he asked.

'Yes, Lord, but Eve gave it to me.' Adam answered. Then Eve added, 'Yes, Lord, but the snake told me I should eat the fruit.'

God was angry with the snake. The snake was really the enemy, Satan. Satan was the one who was really to blame! The enemy's name was Satan. He was jealous of God and wanted to spoil his wonderful world. Now, Adam and Eve could no longer be friends with God. They had disobeyed him and could never again be in the beautiful Garden of Eden. Having eaten the forbidden fruit, they had to leave the Garden.

But God still loved them dearly. He promised everything would one day be well again between God and mankind. He told Eve she would have children, and that some day a baby would be born who would defeat Satan. (God was talking about the Lord Jesus who would be born many years later in Bethlehem.) God then took animal skins and made clothes so that Adam and Eve would not shiver with cold when he sent them away from the garden. To make sure they could never come back he sent an angel to stand guard at the gate.

Cain and Abel

Read: Genesis 4

God no longer allowed Adam and Eve to live in the Garden of Eden. They had been happy there but now life was sad and difficult. It was their own fault because they had disobeyed God. However, one day something happened which made them happy. They had a baby boy who was called Cain. Later another child was born who was called Abel. The little boys grew fast, and soon learned to walk and talk. Adam and Eve taught them about God and that they must love and obey him. As the years passed Cain and Abel grew up and worked hard like their father. Cain became a farmer and Abel a shepherd. They knew that all things came from God. They also knew how to thank God.

When Abel wanted to bring an offering to the Lord he would pick out his best sheep. First he would gather dry branches and sticks which would burn easily. Then he would pile stones together, on top of which he would put all the dry branches he had collected. Then he would kill the sheep and place it carefully on top of the sticks. Abel would then put hot coals under the branches and as soon as the wind caught the flames, the sticks would begin to burn. Because the fire was very hot, the sheep would burn too and the smoke would rise to heaven.

Then Abel would kneel and pray to God. He would present God with an offering of the best of his flock to show God how much he loved him and was thankful to him. The Lord always hears when people pray, and when he heard Abel, he knew that he really loved him and he was happy to receive his offering.

But Cain did not love the Lord. He brought offerings to God and he also prayed, but he wasn't really thankful. He thought, 'Why do I have to thank the Lord? Didn't I plant the wheat myself and didn't I work hard to make it grow?' God saw what was in Cain's heart and he knew that Cain didn't really love him. Because of this, the Lord did not like Cain's offering.

Cain was angry with God and with Abel. He was jealous because God helped Abel. He couldn't understand why God made Abel happy but not him. Cain couldn't get this out of his mind and the more he thought about it the angrier he became. He began to hate his brother and was cruel to him. God warned Cain. 'Cain, why are you so angry and jealous? Isn't it your own fault? If you love me, I will make you happy too, but if you do not love me how can you be happy?' But Cain did not listen and went on doing as he wanted.

One day he said to his brother, 'Let's go to the field.' When they were alone Cain fought with Abel and finally killed him. When Cain saw what he had done he was afraid. He hoped nobody had seen what he had done and he ran away.

But God had seen it! The Lord called out to Cain and asked, 'Where is your brother Abel?'

Cain lied and talked back to God. 'I don't know! I don't have to take care of him, do I?'

God said, 'Because you have done this, I will not allow your wheat to grow on your fields. You must go away, for you may no longer live here. From now on I will have nothing to do with you. No matter where or how far you go, you will never again find rest. Nor will you ever be happy again!'

That is just what happened. Cain went far away from home but he kept thinking about his brother Abel whom he had beaten to death, and was unhappy and afraid for the rest of his life.

Adam and Eve had lost both their sons in one day. When they went out to look for their boys they found Abel lying on the ground. Adam and Eve buried their dead son in the ground. They were very sad but after a while the Lord made them happy again when they had many more sons and daughters. The next baby boy to be born to Adam and Eve was named Seth.

Noah and the Ark

Read: Genesis 6–9

This is the story of a man called Noah who built a wonderful boat. It was very large - over a hundred and forty metres long - and took a long time to build. Noah and his three sons, Shem, Ham and Japheth, built it out of wood. Though there was lots of room for many people, only Noah, his wife, his sons and their wives planned to go on the ship.

Sometimes, when the four men were working, people would come to have a look at the big ship. They would laugh and make fun of Noah and his three sons. 'You can't sail with that ship,' they shouted. 'Can't you see it's standing on dry ground? How can you move such a huge boat to the water?'

'The water will come here!' said Noah. 'There will be water over the entire earth. God has said so. He will punish people because they are so wicked and no longer obey him. Everyone who isn't in the ark when the water comes will drown!' When the people heard this they laughed even louder. 'Don't laugh', said Noah, 'Listen and ask God to forgive you; then you too may come into the ark.'

The people thought this was very funny indeed. They laughed and laughed and laughed. They shouted, 'We're not going to pray to God! Let the water come, we're not afraid!'

They were so bad that they weren't even afraid of punishment. They behaved as though they could do whatever they wanted. In fact, they acted as though there was no God at all. God had been very patient with them and because they wouldn't listen to him, they had to be punished. This is why God had told Noah to build the ark. Noah loved the Lord and neither he nor his wife and children would be punished.

God told Noah exactly how he was to build the ark. There was to be a door here, a window there, and inside there were to be many little rooms. There was to be a good roof over the entire ark, and all the cracks between the planks were to be filled with thick tar so that no water could seep in.

For a long time the people could hear hammering and sawing from early morning until late at night. The people laughed and joked about the boat, and wouldn't listen to Noah's warning of the great flood that was to come.

One day the hammering stopped and the saws were silent. The huge ark was ready. Then God told Noah that he had to put animals, male and female into the ark. They all went in, big and small, each into pens where there was food waiting for them. The people saw all this and wondered what was happening, but they still wouldn't listen. Noah and his family went into the ark and the door was closed. For a week the ark stood waiting, and then... the rains came.

First the sun disappeared as heavy clouds drifted across the sky. Then it began to rain. The big ship stood in the darkness as the rain ran off the roof and streamed down the sides. Soon the water round the ark got deeper and deeper until it floated. Then the wind pushed it along and it began to sail. But where was it going? Noah and the other people in the boat didn't know, but the Lord knew and he steered the boat across the water.

It continued to rain and the water rose higher and higher on the earth. First of all, houses disappeared, then the trees, until finally even the highest mountains were covered. Apart from the fish in the sea, the only life left on earth was in Noah's ark. Everything else had drowned.

God drove the dark clouds away and it stopped raining. Once again the sun began to shine. Nowhere was the earth to be seen. There was only a big deep sea. The eight people on the ark were not afraid because they knew that God would take good care of them. Some day they would all live on the earth again.

For a long time the ark sailed on. Then, without warning, it hit something with a bang and could go no further. It had come to rest on a high mountain and there it was to stay until the earth was dry again. The water was slowly going down, and soon Noah could see the tops of other mountains. It was a long time to wait for Noah and his family, but eventually the water went down.

One day he went to the room in which the birds were roosting, took a big black raven to the window, and set it free. The raven which Noah set free was very happy to be out of the ark and didn't return at the end of the day. Already there was enough food on the water for it to live.

Then Noah let a dove out of the ark. All day long the dove flew back and forth looking for little seeds to eat. But there weren't any seeds to be found and when evening came the dove was very tired and flew back to the ship. It was too soon for the dove to be able to live on the earth. When Noah saw the dove he put his hand out of the window and brought it back into the ark.

Noah waited for a week before he sent the dove out again.

Once more it returned to the boat but this time it brought something with it. The dove brought back a leaf from a tree! It seemed to Noah as though the dove was trying to tell him, 'Look, Noah, it won't be long now, the trees are already out of the water.'

Noah waited for another week and when he freed the dove for the third time it did not come back. It had found food and could now live on the earth too. Then Noah opened the door of the ark and waited for God to speak. Finally, the Lord said, 'Now you may leave the ark with your wife and children and all the animals.'

Noah brought an offering to the Lord. When the smoke rose to heaven, Noah and his family knelt down and thanked God for caring for them during the flood. God saw the offering and saw how pleased and thankful they were. The Lord promised that he would never again send such a great flood to the earth. He said, 'When it rains you do not have to be afraid that I will destroy the whole world. If you look up you will sometimes see my rainbow in the sky. I will also see it and it will be a sign that the world will never again be drowned with a flood.

Abraham and Sarah

Read: Genesis 12 and 13

Once there was a rich man called Abraham. He had many sheep, cattle, donkeys and camels. Abraham had a wife called Sarah. God told him to set off on a long journey with his wife, his relatives, his servants and all his animals.

God said, 'Abraham, you must move to another country. Don't be afraid, for I will show you where it is. I will help the people who are good to you and will punish those who harm you. Your children will live in this new country.' Abraham loved God and when he heard him speaking he did what he was asked to do.

It was a long tiring journey. Abraham's nephew Lot travelled with them. Behind the two men rode Sarah with Lot's wife, and behind them followed all the animals with their little ones. There were also the servants who had to keep the animals together. They went along high mountains and through thick woods. They rode through hot sandy deserts. They passed through many countries which Abraham had never visited before.

Each evening they pitched their tents. The animals, of course, stayed outdoors, where they huddled together and slept, guarded by the servants. Each morning everybody would get up and travel on. Abraham knew the Lord was showing him the way.

One day Abraham came to the country that the Lord had promised. It was called Canaan and God said, 'Abraham, I will give this land to your children and your children's children.' But there was a problem, for Abraham and Sarah had no children.

Although Abraham and Sarah were no longer young, they

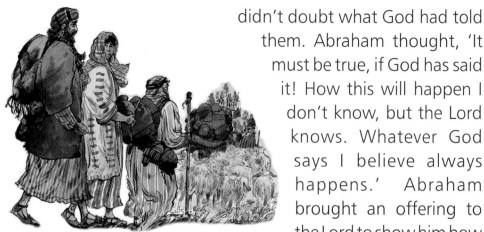

didn't doubt what God had told them. Abraham thought, 'It must be true, if God has said it! How this will happen I don't know, but the Lord knows. Whatever God says I believe always happens.' Abraham brought an offering to the Lord to show him how happy and thankful he was. Then he waited patiently for the time when God would give him and Sarah a baby.

Abraham and his nephew Lot lived happily in that new country, but after a while they realised that they could no longer stay together. Abraham had many sheep and so had Lot. There were hundreds of animals. Each year more young animals were born and the number of the herds kept increasing. Finally the time came when there was no longer enough grass for all of the animals. Lot's servants became angry with the servants of Abraham.

'Go away!' they said. 'This grass is for our sheep!'
'Oh no', replied Abraham's servants, 'this grass is ours!'

Every day there were fresh quarrels and the situation grew worse and worse. Soon Abraham knew that they would have to separate. He took Lot to a high mountain from where they could look out over the whole country. Abraham said, 'Lot, it isn't right that our servants quarrel like this. We had better not stay together. You choose where you want to live. If you choose the country towards the right, I will go towards the left. Or, if you prefer the country to the left, I will go to the right.'

When Lot looked, he saw an area where everything looked lush and green. It was a lovely land with room for many more animals and there was plenty of grass.

In the land which Lot had seen were also two cities. They were called Sodom and Gomorrah and the people who lived there were wicked and godless. Lot didn't seem to mind about this so he chose this beautiful land and moved close to the city of Sodom. Lot had chosen the best land it seemed, but the Lord said to Abraham, 'Don't be sad, Abraham, for later on I will give this entire country to your children. Do you know how many children I will give you? Do you know how many people will live here in the years to come? As many as there are grains of sand on the seashore!'

Many years passed but still Abraham and Sarah had no child from God. At last Sarah said with great sadness, 'Look how old we are; we will probably never have a child now.' Abraham replied, 'Oh yes, we will have a son as God has promised.' But in his heart Abraham was sad at times because it took so long for God to give them the promised child.

One night, God spoke to Abraham and said, 'Don't be sad, Abraham, am I not caring for you?'

Abraham said, 'Oh yes, Lord, but we still have no baby!'

Abraham and Lot

Read: Genesis 12–19

God said to Abraham, 'Look at the sky and count all the stars you can see.' Abraham couldn't do this, of course, because there were far too many stars twinkling in the night. Then God said, 'I shall give you as many children as you see stars in the sky. I will watch over them for they will be my people.'

When Abraham heard this he was happy again, for he believed what the Lord had told him. Knowing these things he could wait longer.

Later, whenever Abraham became sad again, he would look up at the stars and say, 'My child will surely come, for God has promised it. And when that child grows up, he too will have children of his own and more children will be born, until there will be as many people as there are stars in the sky.'

Abraham and Lot no longer lived in the same place. While Abraham lived in a tent in the land of Canaan, Lot went to live in a house in the city of Sodom. One day they both received a message from God. For Abraham it was good news, but for Lot it was bad. It was a hot summer day but beneath the tree where Abraham had pitched his tent it was nice and cool. From a distance came three men. Abraham didn't know them but as they walked towards his home he got up to greet them. When he came close to them, he asked very politely, 'Won't you come into my tent and rest a while. Perhaps you would like something to eat and drink?'

Abraham led them to a resting-place in the shade, the best he could find. He gave them some delicious meat and fresh bread and brought them cold water to drink. Although he didn't know who his guests were he took good care of them. Suddenly, one of the men asked Abraham, 'Where is Sarah, your wife?'

'Over there, in that tent,' replied Abraham, pointing in the direction of her tent.

'Well,' said the visitor, 'a year from now I shall return and Sarah will have a son.'

When Abraham heard this he was very happy. Now he knew who was sitting with him in the shade of the tree. It was the Lord Himself! To think that the Lord with two of his angels, had come to tell him this wonderful news! Sarah did not know the man outside her tent was the Lord. She had been listening from inside the tent but she couldn't believe it. 'Look how old I am,' she said to herself and shook her head and laughed.

'Why did Sarah laugh?' asked the Lord, 'Is anything too hard for God?'

Surprised and afraid, Sarah said quickly, 'I did not laugh.' She lied because she was afraid of being punished. The Lord replied, 'You did laugh, yet what I have told you will surely come to pass.'

The three men had to go and Abraham walked part of the way with them. They came to the top of a high hill, from which they could see the cities of Sodom and Gomorrah. The Lord said, 'Abraham, because you are my friend, I will tell you something. I am going to Sodom and Gomorrah, to see whether the people there still hate God. If they do I must punish and destroy them!'

Abraham was so surprised he couldn't say a word. Was God really going to destroy the two cities? They certainly deserved it, but Lot lived in Sodom and he wasn't godless. He loved the Lord and perhaps there were others like him. Abraham fell on his knees before the Lord and humbly asked, 'Lord, maybe there are some people in Sodom who still love you. Maybe there are fifty, Lord.'

The Lord answered, 'If I find fifty who love me, I will pardon the entire city.'

'And what if there are only forty-five, Lord?' Abraham asked.

'I will still save the city,' said God.

'Maybe there are only forty,' said Abraham.

'Then I will still not punish the city,' said God.

'And if there are only thirty, Lord?'

'Even then I will save the city,' replied God.

'Oh Lord, please do not be angry with me, but perhaps there are only twenty people who still love and serve You.'

And the Lord said, 'If I find twenty, I will not punish the city.'

Abraham hardly dared to ask again, yet he knew how good the Lord was. Very reverently he asked once more, 'Lord, if there are only ten who love you, what then?' And he heard the Lord say, 'If I find ten people in Sodom who love me, I shall not punish the city, because those ten live there!'

When Abraham dared to look up, he found he was alone. In the distance he saw the men walking towards Sodom.

When Lot saw the two strangers coming, he thought, 'I shall take care of those men, for the wicked people of Sodom might harm them.' So he took them to his house, where he gave them supper and invited them to stay for the night.

Suddenly there was a great noise outside! Someone was pounding on the door and there was a great commotion in the street. A voice cried, 'Where are those strangers? We have come to get them; open the door! We'll take care of those strangers for you!' they shouted. The men surrounded the house so that no one could get out. They were such evil men, strangers were not safe in Sodom. Lot went outside and said, 'Don't hurt these men! They have done you no harm.'

But they just ignored Lot and grew angrier. 'Are you telling us what to do? Come here if you dare, and we'll treat you worse than those strangers.'

They almost grabbed Lot but the angels pulled him inside and locked the door.

Then a miracle happened!

The men who wanted to break down the door were struck blind. They looked and looked for the door but it was nowhere to be seen and at last, tired of trying, the men went away. God had kept Lot and his household safe! The angels then told Lot that they were in Sodom to punish the people because of what they had done. They told Lot they were going to destroy the city and all the people in it. It was terrible news!

'But you can be saved, Lot,' said the angels. 'You must go away with your wife and your two daughters.'

Lot could hardly believe the news. What about his house, sheep, cows and other animals? Must he leave them behind? He had worked hard to become rich. Must he give up everything?

However, the day of punishment for Sodom had come! 'Hurry,' said the angels. 'Come, or you too will die!' But Lot didn't seem to hear what they were saying and the angels had to take him by the hand and pull him along. They took his wife and daughters too and when they were outside the city the angels said, 'Now, run for your lives, and don't stand still, don't even look back, for if you do, you will die!'

Only then did they begin to run. Behind them, the ground began to shake and fire fell from heaven. Houses caught fire and the ground was torn open. The entire city disappeared into a hole. Everyone in Sodom died that day but Lot and his two daughters were saved. Sadly, however, Lot's wife was so sorry to have to leave her fine house and all her gold that she turned to look back. She was caught in the destruction and died.

Abraham woke up early that morning and climbed the hill to look toward Sodom. A thick cloud of smoke hung over the land; Sodom was no longer there. It was then that Abraham knew that there weren't even ten people in the whole city who loved the Lord.

Lot went with his two daughters to live somewhere in the mountains. He had wanted so much to be rich, but now he lived in a cave like a poor man. He had loved his house and his gold and his animals, but now he had lost everything.

Hagar and Ishmael

Read: Genesis 16 and 21

A year passed and the baby Abraham and Sarah had been waiting for so long was born. It was a little boy and they called him Isaac. They were very happy, and thankful that this was the child God had promised. He would become the leader of a great people. Little Isaac grew fast. First he learned to crawl around the tent; then he learned to walk and talk. The time came for Abraham to give a party for Isaac who had grown up to be such a big boy.

At the party something happened to spoil the fun. It wasn't Isaac's fault: it was another boy called Ishmael, who also lived with them along with his mother Hagar, one of Abraham and Sarah's servants. Ishmael was much bigger than Isaac and he wasn't very kind to the little boy. Perhaps he was jealous of Isaac and angry? He certainly didn't behave nicely to him. At the party Ishmael teased Isaac. He laughed at him and made fun of him.

Sarah saw Ishmael and said to Abraham, 'You must send that boy away and his mother, too. Ishmael can't stay here with Isaac for he always wants to be the leader and he is very mean to Isaac.'

Abraham loved Ishmael and Hagar and didn't want to send them away, but eventually Hagar and Ishmael left Abraham's tent, taking with them loaves of bread and a bottle of cold water. Hagar and Ishmael had to walk a long way and soon they were lost in the hot and sandy desert. As far as the eye could see there was nothing but sand. There wasn't even a tree to give them shade and it was so hot they grew very thirsty. Further and further they wandered. But even though they had no one to take care of them God saw them and he looked after them.

As they wandered on Ishmael became very tired. Hagar gave him another drink of water but the bottle was almost empty. Ishmael could hardly walk another step. 'Please, mother, I'm so thirsty!' Hagar put the bottle to his lips again but it was empty! 'There's no more water!' he cried.

Hagar was startled. She looked round to see if she could find a well or a stream, but there was nothing. There wasn't even a puddle. There was nothing but hot dry sand. Ishmael was so thirsty that he could walk no further and fell down. He lay on the sand, groaning with pain. Hagar didn't know what to do. She picked her child up and took him over to a small bush which she hoped would give him a little shade. There was nothing else she could do.

Ishmael lay there with his eyes closed and his moaning grew softer and softer. Hagar couldn't watch any longer, for she couldn't bear to see her child die. She walked a little way away, sat down in the sand and cried.

'Oh, my boy,' she sobbed. 'My darling boy, you are dying of thirst, and I can't help you!' The tears ran down her cheeks to the burning hot sand. Then all at once Hagar looked up. She looked around but saw no one; yet a voice spoke to her, 'Hagar, what is the matter? Don't be afraid. I have heard the boy's cry. I will take care of him.'

Hagar knew this voice well, for it was the voice of God! Now everything would be all right. Quickly she dried her tears and ran to her child. There she saw a well, a deep hole in the ground with sparkling clear water in it. She ran to the well with her water bottle and filled it right to the top. Then she hurried to her boy, held him up and put the bottle to his lips.

Ishmael drank deeply and he opened his eyes. His pale cheeks grew rosy again and, after a while, he was able to get up and walk.

Now they both knew there was somebody who cared for them. Father Abraham wasn't there, but their Father in heaven was and he would always stay close to them. The Lord showed Hagar the way to the country where they would live.

There Ishmael grew into a big strong man. He grew into a good hunter. Every day he hunted in the desert. All his life, he knew that the Lord cared for him.

Abraham's big test

Read: Genesis 22

Isaac had grown up and Abraham loved him more and more every day. Abraham also loved God, for it was God who had given him the child. But whom did Abraham love the most, God or Isaac? Abraham often brought offerings to the Lord, which he gave with great reverence and adoration. He would be willing to give God everything he had.

One night God spoke to Abraham: 'You must give your child to me. You must offer him to me on Mount Moriah.'

Abraham was shocked! How could God ask him to sacrifice the son that God had given him and whom he loved so dearly? Hadn't God said that Isaac would live in this land and become the father of a great nation? Abraham didn't understand it but God had said it, and Abraham had to obey and have faith that all would turn out well in the end.

The next morning Abraham got up very early, saddled a donkey, and called two of his servants before going to the tent where Isaac slept.

'Wake up, my boy, we're going on a long journey.' But he didn't tell him what was going to happen.

This sounded wonderful to Isaac. It was probably the most exciting trip Isaac had ever had in his life. It took three days to reach the mountain. However, for Abraham it was the saddest journey he had ever made.

Abraham told his servants, 'You wait here with the donkey. Isaac and I are going a little further. When we have made the offering we will return.'

He really meant it too, because he believed that the Lord would make everything right. Isaac carried the wood, while Abraham carried a pot with burning coals in it. As the two were going up the mountain, Isaac stopped and asked, 'Father, you have the fire and I'm carrying the wood, but where is the lamb we will offer to God?'

Abraham replied, 'The Lord will provide a lamb, my son.' So the two went on together.

When they reached the top of the mountain, Abraham built the altar of stones. He placed the wood on it... then Abraham had to explain. He told Isaac he must be the sacrifice. Putting ropes round Isaac, he placed him on the altar.

Just as Abraham raised the knife a voice said, 'Abraham! Abraham!' God had seen how willingly Abraham would give everything he had. Abraham replied gladly, 'Here I am!'

Then the Lord said, 'Stop, don't hurt the boy! Now I know you love me above all else. You are even willing to give me your only child!'

Abraham cut the ropes from Isaac and, taking him in his arms, he held him tight. Suddenly a rustling noise came from behind him and he saw a ram caught by its horns in the bushes. God had provided a sacrifice! Abraham put the animal on the wood and gave the Lord an offering. Then they went home together. God had made everything work out well in the end. Isaac would become the father of a great people.

Jacob and Esau

Read: Genesis 25 and 27

Isaac became a great man. He lived in the tent of his father, Abraham, and he was the master over everything. Both Abraham and Sarah had died. Isaac didn't live in his father's tent alone. He had a wife whose name was Rebekah and they had two children, Jacob and Esau. Jacob and Esau were twins, but Esau was just a little bit older as he was born first. Although they were twins they did not look at all alike. Esau's skin was hairy. Jacob's skin was smooth and fair.

Esau was a rough boy, full of life. When he grew older, it was hard for him to stay at home for any length of time. He often went far into the fields and woods, where he hunted deer and other wild animals. Jacob was quieter, and was content to stay in the tent with his mother, or care for the sheep. Jacob loved God and wanted to be his child.

Esau wasn't a godly man yet Isaac loved Esau more than he loved Jacob. Esau often brought home good meat from his hunting trips. He would cook it just the way Isaac liked it. On the other hand, Rebekah loved Jacob more than his brother. He would stay at home with her and talk with her like a grown man. But which of the two would later live in Isaac's tent, take care of the sheep, goats and other animals? Who was to receive from Isaac the special blessing of the eldest son? Remember, Esau was the first-born.

However, Isaac and Rebekah knew, because God had told them it was to be Jacob. Rebekah was pleased with this but Isaac thought he knew better than God. He said, 'Esau is the eldest, and the eldest must receive the special blessing.' Rebekah often thought about the blessing and so did Jacob because he knew that Esau was the elder.

One day Jacob was sitting in front of his tent. He had cooked some lentil soup over a fire and the delicious smell was carried out over the fields on the breeze. Esau had been out hunting all day long and he was very tired and hungry. When he smelled the soup his eyes sparkled and he called out to his brother, 'Give me some of that soup you have there!'

Jacob looked at him slyly and replied, 'You may have it, provided you allow me to be called the elder brother so that I can get the special blessing.'

Esau laughed and answered, 'What do I care about such things; of course you may!' And so Esau got his lentil soup and Jacob was to get the special blessing but Jacob really had not done the right thing.

Many years passed, and Isaac grew old. He became weak and finally went completely blind. Each day, as he lay on his bed in the tent, he wondered, 'Who will be the master over everything after I die? Surely I will die before long; then who will live in my tent? It must be Esau!' So One day he called Esau and said, 'My son, go to the forest and hunt for a deer. Prepare it just the way I like it. Then, after I have eaten, I will give you the special blessing.' Esau left for the woods to hunt for a deer. Now, Esau should have said, 'No father, Jacob must have the blessing, for I promised it to him many years ago.' But instead he thought, 'What do I care about the promise to Jacob. I would like to have the blessing for myself.'

Rebekah overheard all this through the tent wall and she ran to Jacob immediately. 'We have to act quickly', she said, 'if you are to have the blessing. We must deceive your father. Run to the flock and bring me two small goats. I will cook them just the way your father likes them; then you must bring them to him. Your father is blind and you must act just like Esau, so that he won't know the difference.'

But Jacob was afraid. 'Father can feel that I'm not Esau,' he said. 'My hands are soft and smooth, while Esau's are rough and hairy.'

Rebekah had the answer to this. 'Just do as I tell you,' she said, 'and I will take care of all these things.'

So Jacob did as he was told. First he killed the two goats and gave them to Rebekah to cook. Then she gave him Esau's best suit to wear, which had the smell of the woods and fields on them. Cutting the skin of the young goats, she fitted them to Jacob's hands and neck and then sent him to his father's tent.

'Father,' he said.

'Who are you, my son?'

'I am Esau, your eldest boy. I have come back from the woods, with the meat you asked for. Sit up and eat what I have prepared for you; then give me your blessing.'

Isaac noticed something wrong. He said, 'Are you really Esau? You have such a strange voice; come here and let me touch you. Let me feel whether or not you really are Esau.'

Jacob knelt down beside the bed so that Isaac could feel his hands. 'The voice is Jacob's, but the hands are Esau's,' said the old man. Softly he asked just once more, 'Are you really Esau?'

'Yes,' lied Jacob, 'I'm really Esau.'

The meat was beside the bed and it smelled delicious. Isaac ate some then Jacob gave him some wine to drink too. Isaac said, 'Kiss me, my son.' When Jacob bent close to his father, Isaac could smell the clothes of Esau. Smelling the woods and fields in the cloth he was sure it was Esau kneeling beside the bed. Reaching over, he placed his hands on Jacob's head. In doing this, he blessed him and told Jacob that one

day he would be the master of
all the house. He told him he
would be the friend of God.
Jacob didn't dare look up. He
felt awfully guilty, because he
had cheated his old father.

Nevertheless he had received the blessing, just as God said would happen.

A little while later Esau came home. He had killed the deer his father had asked for and had come to clean and cook it. When it was ready he brought it in to his father's tent. 'Father, here I am,' he called.

Isaac's heart pounded. Suddenly he knew he had been deceived. Esau shook with anger when he heard about the trick his brother had played. He told everyone, 'When my father is gone, I shall kill Jacob. I will kill that liar!'

Rebekah heard this and she called to Jacob, 'You must go away quickly and live with your uncle in a country far away. When Esau is no longer so angry with you, I'll let you know.'

And so Jacob ran away from his family to hide where his brother Esau couldn't find him. Now he was a poor homeless wanderer because he had lied to his father and Esau. Rebekah lost the boy she loved so much and Isaac was sad too as he lay on his bed.

Jacob makes a new life for himself

Read: Genesis 28 and 29

Jacob went far away from his home. He didn't want to go but he was afraid of his brother after he had tricked him. It was a long journey to the land where his uncle lived and Jacob felt both lonely and sad.

He was sorry for having lied to his blind old father. Jacob thought, 'No one cares about me any more. Maybe even God no longer cares, because I have been so bad.' This was the worst thought of all - to think God might be angry with him and no longer be his friend. Evening came and the sun set. It became quite dark and there was no house where Jacob might sleep. He would have to sleep outdoors under the open sky. He lay down on the ground and rested his head on a stone. As he lay there, looking up at the stars, God was not very far away. Surely God would never again look at Jacob, the deceiver.

Jacob thought to himself, 'If only the Lord would forgive me. How sorry I am for what I have done; I want so much to be his friend.' Then he fell asleep. While Jacob slept, he had a strange dream. In the dream he saw a long ladder which reached up to heaven. Angels walked up and down the ladder.

At the very top of the ladder was the Lord God himself who said, 'I am the Lord, the God of Abraham and of Isaac your father. Don't be afraid! Go on your way, for I am going with you and I will also bring you back safely. You may still be my friend. Many years from now your children will live in this very land where you are now sleeping.'

Jacob woke up. He had been dreaming for a long time and it was morning. He remembered the dream. The Lord had said that he would care for Jacob and so he wanted to mark the spot where he had slept. He used the stone on which he had rested his head as a memorial. He wanted to show God how thankful he was so he took a small jar of oil that he had with him and poured it on the stone as an offering, praying, 'Lord, thank you for being so good to me. I want to love you always and when I return to this place I will bring another offering.' No longer feeling

afraid or lonely he travelled on his way. God went with him and looked after him, bringing him safely to his uncle's home.

Jacob returns

Read: Genesis 29–33

Jacob became the servant of his uncle in the far away land. He took care of his uncle's sheep and his cattle. When he was there he married Leah, one of his uncle's daughters. Later he married another daughter called Rachel, and he had many children. Jacob stayed with his uncle for a long time. He worked hard and became a rich man with his own sheep, cattle and other animals.

Many years ago, Jacob's mother had said, 'I will let you know when you may come back. I will tell you when Esau is no longer angry with you.' He waited but his mother did not get in touch.

One day God said, 'Jacob, you must go back to your own country. I am going with you. I will take care of you.'

Jacob prepared for the long trip. He took his wives and children, his servants and his sheep, his cattle and his camels. It was a long parade of people and animals, just like Abraham's procession to Canaan so many years before.

Jacob had fled from Canaan all alone. Now he was returning a very rich man, with children and servants and animals that all belonged to him. How well the Lord had taken care of him.

At first his uncle didn't want to let Jacob go to Canaan. But the Lord told him, 'You must let Jacob go.'

It was a long, tiring trip but finally Jacob came close to the land where he had lived as a child. Jacob grew afraid when he remembered how angry Esau had been. Would Esau remember? Would he still be angry? He hoped not, because Esau was strong and rough. If he was still angry with Jacob and wanted to fight, Jacob would lose! Jacob thought to himself, 'I know what I'll do. I'll send Esau a message that I want to be friends.' So he sent Esau a gift of sheep, goats and camels. It was a very big herd of animals; a few servants went ahead to present them to Esau.

When the servants returned they said, 'Master, be careful! Esau is coming with many strong men. All of them have swords and spears with which to fight.' Jacob was afraid because he thought Esau was coming to kill them all. He was so terrified he couldn't sleep. Long after all the others were in bed he remained outside in the dark night. It was there in the night that he met with God. God blessed him and gave him a new name, Israel.

Then Esau came. The ground shook as Esau rode towards Jacob with all his servants. Clouds of dust blew up into the air. It seemed very dangerous but Jacob was no longer afraid. Calmly he walked over to Esau; then, to his surprise, Esau put his strong arms around Jacob and kissed him! He wasn't angry at all, but glad that his brother had come back at last.

The Lord had taken all the anger out of Esau's heart. The two brothers sat down and talked together, for they had a lot to talk about. It was a wonderful day. The children all came over to kiss their uncle Esau. Before evening came, Esau left and Jacob travelled on to the land of Canaan until finally he reached his home. He learned that his mother Rebekah had died since he left home, but that his father Isaac was still living and was very happy that his son had returned. Later, after Isaac died, Jacob went to live in his father's tent.

Joseph and his jealous brothers

Read: Genesis 37

Jacob had many children. One was called Joseph. He had ten older brothers and one younger than himself. The little brother's name was Benjamin and his father loved him very much. But Jacob loved Joseph even more than Benjamin. As a matter of fact, he loved Joseph more than all his other sons.

Once he gave Joseph a beautiful coat with many colours in it. It was magnificent. Most of the time Benjamin stayed at home with his father and Joseph while the other brothers were out in the field looking after the animals. Sometimes Joseph would help his brothers, but it wasn't much fun, as they were always jealous of him because he had received such a beautiful coat from their father.

One night Joseph had a dream that he was with his brothers in the wheat fields. The wheat had been cut but it had to be tied up in bundles called sheaves. In his dream Joseph bound a sheaf and laid it on the ground. Suddenly his sheaf stood upright and the sheaves of his brothers bowed down to it. Joseph couldn't forget this dream. He told his brothers about it but they got very angry and said, 'You'd really like that, wouldn't you? You'd love us all to bow before you and make you our ruler! It'll never happen, you silly dreamer!' Then Joseph had another strange dream. He dreamt that the sun, the moon and eleven stars bowed before him. Even his father scolded him when he told the others about it. Jacob asked him, 'What foolishness is this?' But Joseph couldn't explain the dream.

Joseph's dreams made all his brothers very angry. After a while, they became so angry they wanted to kill him. Fortunately, they didn't dare beat him to death as their father was nearby.

One day the brothers took the sheep a long way from home and didn't come back when they were supposed to. Finally Jacob said to Joseph, 'You had better look for your brothers and see if they're all right, I'm worried about them. When you find them come back quickly and tell me how they are.'

So Joseph went out to look for his brothers. When they saw him coming they planned to attack him. 'Look', they said, 'here comes the dreamer, and father isn't here! Now that we have him, we'll kill him, and throw his body into that deep hole over there. We will tell father that a wild animal attacked him. Then we'll see what will come of all those fine dreams!'

But the oldest brother Reuben said, 'No. Don't kill him! Throw him into the hole alive.' Reuben wasn't as bad as the others but he was afraid of them. He thought he could outsmart them, and save Joseph by returning when it was dark to rescue him out of the horrible pit.

The brothers grabbed Joseph, tore off his beautiful coat and threw him into the hole. They had absolutely no pity for him and didn't listen when he cried out in fear.

'Just lie there and keep on dreaming that you're our leader!' Then they sat down close to the pit and ate their lunch, while their younger brother was crying in the hole next to them.

Reuben, however, wasn't quite so cruel. He took a walk in the field and thought, 'Just wait, Joseph, as soon as it's dark I'll come and help you.' Reuben thought he had fooled his brothers.

It was a good thing for Joseph that there wasn't any water in the old well. He was safe from drowning but he couldn't get out because the walls were too steep and slippery. Jacob, of course, was far away and knew nothing about what was going on.

Suddenly Joseph heard voices, and there were his brothers at the mouth of the pit. They had come to pull him out with a rope. But when they pulled him out he noticed that there were strange men with them, and camels with packs on their backs. They looked like traders from another country, and they were giving money to his brothers. Suddenly Joseph realised what was happening! His brothers had sold him as a slave. They took Joseph, tied him up and put him on to a camel. He looked back at his brothers and called out, 'Help me, please help me! I want to go home to my father.'

But the brothers paid no attention and Reuben wasn't there to help. Later, long after Joseph and the traders were out of sight, Reuben came back, but it was too late. 'Now what?' asked Reuben. 'What will our father say about this?' The other brothers had planned it carefully and knew exactly what to do.

They were wicked and not afraid to make up a false story. First they killed a goat and poured its blood on Joseph's beautiful coat. Then they took the coat to Jacob saying, 'Look, father, we found this in the field. Isn't this Joseph's coat?' When Jacob saw the coat he thought Joseph had been killed by a wild animal and the poor old man was heartbroken.

Jacob said, 'I will never be happy again, now that my dear Joseph is dead!' He didn't know, of course, that the blood on the coat was only goat's blood.

Joseph in Egypt

Read: Genesis 39–40

Jacob believed that Joseph was dead. But he was alive in the country of Egypt where the traders had sold him to a rich man called Potiphar. Joseph was a slave and could not go home to his father no matter how much he wanted to. Potiphar's servants had to work hard all day. If one was lazy, or complained, he was punished. Joseph was not lazy, nor did he complain. Instead he tried hard to do his best.

He thought, 'God still sees me, even in this far country. God wants me to do the best I can.' Everything went well, for God took good care of Joseph. He blessed him and helped him do his work. Joseph turned out to be the best servant in Potiphar's household. Potiphar noticed this and said to him one day, 'Joseph, you may be the head over all my servants and everything I have.' Joseph was free to go anywhere he wished in the house.

Now Potiphar's wife was rather sly. One day she tried to trick Joseph into doing wrong. But Joseph said, 'I cannot do that. God sees everything we do. Do you think I would do this sin against God?' So he refused to obey her. But every time she saw Joseph she spoke about it. She wouldn't leave him alone. One day, when Potiphar was away, she grabbed Joseph by his coat and pulled him towards her. 'You must do as I say!' she said.

Joseph pulled himself free and ran away but he left his coat behind him in her hands. She began to scream and cry, 'Help, help, Joseph attacked me!' Other servants came running and believed her, because they saw Joseph's coat in her hands. When Potiphar came home he listened to his wife and he believed her too. He was so angry that he had Joseph thrown into prison along with thieves, murderers and other evil men. Joseph had done nothing wrong, yet he was still being punished. But the Lord saw him there and said, 'Do not be afraid, Joseph. Be patient. I love you and I will take care of you even here in prison.' Joseph wasn't alone. God was still with him, he knew Joseph had done nothing wrong.

It didn't take long before the Jailor realised that Joseph could be trusted. Joseph was put in charge of the other prisoners and again he worked hard and God blessed him in everything he did, but he remained a prisoner and was not free to leave.

One day two new prisoners were brought in. They were important men. One was the king's cup-bearer. He used to pour the king's wine and serve it to him. The other man was the baker for the king. They had both been put in prison because the king was angry with them.

Every morning Joseph gave them their food, but one day when he opened their door, they sat staring and afraid. 'What's the matter?' Joseph asked.

'Oh!' they said. 'We had strange dreams and we don't know what they mean.'

'What did you dream about?' asked Joseph.

The cup-bearer described his dream first. 'I dreamt that I was out of prison. I saw a beautiful vine which had three branches. The branches were loaded with big luscious grapes. In my hand I held the golden cup of the king. I pressed the juice out of the grapes and let it run into the cup and then I brought the cup of wine to the king.'

While Joseph listened the Lord told him the meaning of the dream. He said, 'The three branches are three days. At the end of three days you will be free and you will again be the cup-bearer of the king.'

Then Joseph asked him, 'Will you ask the king if I may also be set free? I have done no wrong either.'

'Of course!' the cup-bearer promised. He would promise anything if only he could be free again.

Then the baker wanted to tell Joseph his dream.

'I also dreamt I was out of prison again. I walked in the street with three baskets on my head, one on top of the other. In the top basket were delicious cakes for the king, but the birds came and picked at the cakes and ate everything up.'

Joseph looked very sad and said, 'This dream does not bring good news. Those three baskets also mean three days, but in those three days the king will punish you for doing wrong. He will kill you and hang your body from a tree, where the birds will come and pick at your flesh.'

And all these things happened just as Joseph had told them. Three days later the cup-bearer was free and the baker was punished.

But the cup-bearer forgot all about his promise to Joseph. He was so glad to be out of prison he didn't even think about his time there. Joseph waited and waited but no one came to take him out of prison. But God hadn't forgotten him, although he had to stay in prison for another two years before being released. This is how it happened.

Joseph becomes the King's Governor

Read: Genesis 41

One night when Joseph was still in prison the king had a strange dream. He dreamt that he was standing near the river, when out of the water came seven fat cattle. They began to eat the grass on the river bank. Then seven more came out of the water but they were skinny. All at once the thin cattle went over to the fat ones and began to eat them. They ate them all up yet the skinny ones didn't get any fatter. Even though they ate the big fat ones the skinny cattle remained just as thin as before.

The king was so startled he woke up. Realising it was just a dream, he fell asleep again and had another strange dream. This time he saw a tiny wheat plant with seven round ears full of kernels. Another plant began to grow and this also had seven ears, but they were thin and empty, with no kernels in them at all. The same thing happened as with the cattle. The empty ears bent over the full ears and ate them.

The king woke up again, but this time he couldn't sleep any longer. He called his servants and told them what he had dreamt.

'Surely this means something!' he said. 'Explain it to me.'

But none of his servants knew what it meant. With the other servants was the cup-bearer who suddenly remembered Joseph and told the king about him.

'Bring Joseph to me right now,' said the king.

Joseph was taken out of prison, washed and given new clothes before being taken to the king. The king asked, 'Can you tell me the meaning of these dreams?'

'No, my king,' Joseph replied. 'Only God knows the meaning of dreams. He will tell me.'

Then the king told Joseph the dream of the seven fat and seven thin cattle and the seven ears full of wheat and seven empty ones.

Joseph explained, 'These two dreams mean the same thing.

First there will be seven very good years. During this time much wheat will grow on the land. Following this there will be seven bad years, when nothing will grow. The people will then have nothing to eat.'

'Oh,' said the king. 'Then we will die of hunger?'

'No, my king,' replied Joseph. 'You must build warehouses

and have the people fill them with wheat. In the seven good years there will be plenty. When the bad years come, you will have food for all the people.'

'Oh good,' shouted the king. 'This will indeed be done. How wise and sensible you are, Joseph. You had better take charge of all these matters and of the people of my country. You may do whatever you like. I am the only one over you. I am the king, but you are the governor.'

He took his gold ring and put it on Joseph's finger. He gave him fine clothes to wear and put a gold chain around his neck. Joseph rode in one of the king's coaches through the city. All the people had to bow before Joseph as though he were the king himself. He was given a beautiful house to live in with many servants and all kinds of attractive things. He had become a very wealthy and important man. But Joseph did not become proud even though he had all these wonderful things. He knew who had really given him all this. Joseph was happy and very thankful.

Joseph's brothers go to Egypt

Read: Genesis 42–45

Everything happened just as Joseph had said. First came the seven good years. The people couldn't eat all the crops they had grown so they brought the surplus to Joseph who stored it in big barns. Then the seven bad years came when nothing would grow. The sun was so hot that the plants burned and died. Everywhere in the world people were hungry, but in Egypt, there was plenty to eat. Joseph even began to sell grain to people from other countries.

One day ten men came to Joseph to buy grain. Joseph couldn't help but stare when he saw who the men were. They were his brothers who had been so cruel to him long ago! Joseph remembered them very well indeed. After all, they had sold him as a slave. Joseph knew them immediately but they didn't recognise him. They knelt down before him, the dignified governor. Joseph's dream of long ago had come true!

If he had wanted, Joseph could have punished them there and then for the terrible things they had done to him. He could have had them killed or thrown in prison. But Joseph wasn't angry with his brothers even though they had caused him so much grief. He wanted to forgive them and to be kind to them. But he didn't tell them who he was. First of all he wanted to find out where Benjamin was. So he said, 'Where did you come from?'

'From the land of Canaan, sir,' they replied. They told him of their old father and a younger brother who had stayed at home. They also told him they were all very hungry. As the governor,

Joseph made himself look angry and said, 'I don't believe you. You are lying! You are enemies who have come to spy on us and later you will come with an army to steal all we have.'

'No, no sir,' they protested. 'We are honest men who have come to buy grain because we are very hungry!'

Joseph pretended not to believe them. 'Go home and fetch your youngest brother, then I will believe you. To make sure you will come back one of you must remain here.'

So Simeon remained behind as a hostage while the others went back home. Joseph had their bags filled and loaded on to the donkeys and then they left. The brothers felt sad and afraid. They had got what they wanted but Simeon had had to stay behind in Egypt. Jacob was afraid something awful would happen to Benjamin if he allowed him to go to Egypt so he wouldn't allow them to take him back to the angry governor.

However, as the weeks passed, the supply of grain began to be used up. Finally, they had to go back to Egypt for more, but the brothers didn't dare go there without Benjamin. They knew that the governor would be very angry if they didn't bring Benjamin and they were afraid for Simeon. It was a desperate situation and finally Judah spoke up and said to Jacob, 'Allow me to take Benjamin, father. I will see no harm is done to him. I will take care of him.'

'All right,' said Jacob. 'Take him. I will pray for God to take care of you all.'

Together the ten brothers set off for Egypt, where everything went much better than they had dared to hope.

When they arrived they were taken to the palace where they saw Simeon. The governor was very friendly indeed. Joseph was extremely happy to see Benjamin. He was so happy he began to cry and hurried into another room so that the brothers couldn't see his tears. Eventually he went back to speak with his brothers.

He invited them to eat at the palace. Benjamin came too and he was given the best food and the largest helping. They also had delicious wine to drink. Joseph drank from a very fine silver cup.

Later, in the middle of the night, when the brothers were sleeping, Joseph had the empty bags filled again, but this time the silver cup was secretly slipped into Benjamin's sack.

Next morning they set out for home with food for their families. All had gone well with Benjamin and they had Simeon with them too. They walked fast to get home to Jacob as soon as possible with the good news.

Suddenly they heard shouting! A band of soldiers came running after them. The first soldier shouted, 'Stop! Wait there! Why have you stolen the governor's silver cup?'

The brothers were frightened at first but then they grew angry. They said, 'What do you think we are? Thieves? We haven't stolen anything. Search our bags! You may do what you like with the man who has the governor's silver cup.'

'All right,' said the soldiers. 'The one who has the cup goes back with us to the governor.'

So the soldiers looked and found the silver cup in Benjamin's sack. 'I didn't steal the cup. I don't know how it got into my bag!' cried Benjamin. No matter how much he protested it did no good. The soldiers grabbed him and took him back with them. The brothers wouldn't leave Benjamin at a time like this so they also went back. When they all stood before the governor he was stern and angry, just as he had been the first time they came.

'Go away,' he said to the brothers. 'Benjamin is the only one who has to stay here.' But the brothers wouldn't go! They loved their youngest brother, and Judah cared for him the most. Judah said, 'Sir, please let Benjamin go home! Our old father will die broken-hearted if something happens to him. Let Benjamin go and punish me. I promised father I would take care of him.'

Then Joseph knew his brothers had changed. He had to tell

them who he really was and sobbed aloud, 'I am Joseph! I am Joseph!' Then he asked, 'Is my father still alive?' Never had the brothers been so surprised! Could it be possible this was the same Joseph whom they had teased so much, the one they had sold to the traders? Was Joseph really the stern governor they were facing at this moment? They shook with fear because they were afraid that he would get even with them for the things they had done.

'Don't be afraid,' Joseph told them. 'I am not angry with you anymore. You have done wrong but God has made all things right again, and I have forgiven you everything. Had I not come to Egypt you wouldn't have had any food for your families.'

He kissed Benjamin and all the others and then he sent them home quickly to Jacob. He also gave them fine presents to take along including a coach for Jacob to ride in. He told them, 'You must come back with my father and live here in Egypt. I will see that you always have enough food to eat.'

Everything had turned out well. No soldiers came after them this time to take them back to the governor and the journey home was a happy one.

Jacob comes to Egypt

Read: Genesis 46–47

Jacob was standing near his tent as he watched for his sons' return. He was pleased to see them all, including Benjamin. God had heard his prayer. 'Father, Joseph is still alive!' they called out to him as they came closer. 'He is the governor in Egypt!' Jacob's face became pale with shock. He couldn't believe his dearest son, Joseph, was still alive. Could it be possible that he was now such a great man?

But when his sons showed him the lovely presents and the beautiful coach Joseph had sent, Jacob had to believe them. He laughed and cried at the same time. 'My son Joseph is still alive and I will see him before I die,' he cried.

Shortly after this they all went on the long journey to Egypt. Judah went ahead to tell Joseph his father was coming. When Jacob came close to Egypt, Joseph rode out to meet him. As soon as he saw his father, he jumped from the coach, ran, threw his arms around him and kissed him.

'Joseph, my dear, dear son,' said Jacob. They both cried for joy. 'Now that I have seen you again,' said Jacob, 'I can die in peace.'

Jacob settled with all his children in the land of Egypt, where Joseph was governor. They moved to a part of the country called Goshen. Joseph had saved them all from death for, had he not been the governor of Egypt, they would have died from hunger during the famine. Now they were all in Egypt and they all lived happily together.

Moses in the Basket

Read: Exodus 1–2

Long after Jacob and his sons had died, there lived a father and mother in the land of Goshen. They had three children. The first was a girl called Miriam. The second was a boy whose name was Aaron. The third was a baby boy. Amram and Jochabed were very upset when the new baby came because they knew that they would not be allowed to keep him. A new king was now ruling the land, who knew nothing about Joseph.

He didn't know that Joseph had saved Egypt from hunger and death. Jacob, Joseph and all his brothers had died but their children had remained in Goshen. At first they had been a small group, but as time went by more babies were born. The children grew into men and women who also had children, and now they had become a great nation, called the children of Israel, which was another name given to Jacob.

The new king was very afraid of the people of Israel. He thought, 'Those people are growing too strong. Soon they will be stronger than the Egyptians and then they will try to rule us. This must never happen.'

This was why all the baby boys who were born to the Israelites were to be drowned. The people must not grow too large or too strong. To keep their numbers down he ordered that all the baby boys were to be thrown into the river Nile.

Amram and Jochabed loved their baby so much and couldn't do this dreadful thing. Besides, they knew God wouldn't want them to do it.

They hid their new baby in a dark corner of the house so that no one would find him. They warned Miriam and Aaron, 'You must not tell anyone you have a baby brother! If the king should hear about it he will send soldiers to take our baby away and throw him into the river.' Miriam and Aaron kept the secret.

The baby's father had to work for the king. Early each morning he and all the other men in Goshen had to go and make bricks. With the bricks they built walls, houses and palaces. They had to build an entire city. Whoever didn't work hard enough was beaten. The people grumbled about it but it didn't help at all as the king was their master.

Nobody knew there was a baby boy in the little house in Goshen. His mother kept him safe for three long months. Sometimes the baby would cry long and hard and as he grew stronger, his cry became louder. He could be heard out in the street and it became very hard to hide him. The soldiers walked up and down the streets outside the houses so the parents were afraid that they would hear the baby and take him away.

Then they had an idea. Jochabed went down to the river where she picked twigs and reeds from along the bank. Then she took them home where she wove them into a basket. She closed the cracks between the reeds with pitch until it looked like a cradle. When it was finished she put the baby inside and took the basket outdoors. Miriam went with her mother to the river where the Egyptians drowned the baby boys. Wading into the water she carefully placed the basket between the reeds at the river's edge, where the water wasn't very deep.

The little basket now looked like a small boat as it floated on the water. In the basket lay the baby, fast asleep. The mother then left her baby in the rushes under the care of God. For it was God alone who would really protect the little boy. Then Jochabed went home, leaving Miriam hiding in the bushes where she could keep an eye on the basket with her baby brother.

Then Miriam heard voices and footsteps. She peeped through the bushes to see who was coming. She saw a beautiful lady strolling along with her maids. It was the princess, the daughter of the king. It was a very warm day and she was looking for a nice place to bathe in the cool water of the river. As she walked along the riverbank she saw the basket.

'Oh, look! What is that? Go and fetch it for me,' she ordered. One of her maids went into the water to get the basket and, just as she picked it up, the baby woke and started to cry. When the princess saw the crying baby she felt sorry for it.

'What a dear little baby,' she said. 'It must be a little boy of the people of Israel, but this one won't be drowned. I have found him and he will become my son. I shall call him Moses; a good name for him, because it means "Taken out of the water".'

All this time the baby kept crying because he was hungry and needed his mother's milk. The princess couldn't nurse him, nor could her maids. Just then Miriam came out of the bushes. She had heard everything they had said and asked, 'Shall I get a woman who can nurse the baby?'

'Please do,' said the princess. 'Go quickly.'

Miriam ran fast and called her mother. When they returned, the princess asked, 'Will you nurse this baby?'

'Yes, princess,' said Jochabed.

'Take him home with you then. Keep him and take good care of him. I will pay you until he is older and can feed himself. Then I must have him back as my son.'

'Very well, princess,' said Moses' mother.

God had heard their prayers and had cared for the baby. Moses would live and Jochabed would even receive money to look after him. She no longer had to hide Moses in a dark corner, nor be afraid that the soldiers would come and take him away. Everyone in the family was happy because of what God had done for them.

Moses becomes a Prince

Read: Exodus 2

Moses stayed with his mother for some time. He played with his brother and sister and learned all about the children of Israel. Later Moses had to move to the palace and be brought up as an Egyptian. Now the princess was his mother and Moses became a prince. He was given different clothes and lived in a palace.

But Moses remembered the wonderful stories that his real mother had told him about the God of Israel. Moses knew that he didn't really belong to the Egyptians, he belonged to the people of Israel, the people of God!

One day Moses went for a walk to the neighbourhood where he was born. The Egyptians continued to force the Israelites to make bricks and build houses. Whoever didn't work hard enough was beaten. Suddenly he heard a man cry out. He was being whipped by a cruel Egyptian. No matter how loudly the poor man cried the Egyptian paid no attention and had no pity on him.

Moses was angry with what he saw. Looking around quickly, he saw that no one was close by so he jumped on top of the Egyptian and beat him to death.

Now the Egyptian could never again harm the people of Israel, for he lay dead on the ground. But Moses knew that he had to move the body for no one must know what he had done. As fast as he could, Moses dug a hole in the ground, put the man in it and filled it with sand as if nothing had happened. When he went for a walk the next day he heard shouting. Was someone else being beaten by another Egyptian? But this time it was two men of Israel quarrelling and fighting.

He tried to stop the fight but one of the men looked at him rudely and said, "It is none of your business. You are not our boss." Then he added, "Maybe you want to kill me as you killed the Egyptian?" Moses was shocked when he heard this. Perhaps everybody knew about it now?

When the King heard of it he tried to have Moses killed so Moses fled to the desert where he thought no one would find him. He had wanted to help the children of Israel but there seemed to be nothing that he could do now. God alone could help the people of Israel. Moses had to wait quietly for God's time.

Moses becomes a Shepherd

Read: Exodus 2 and 3

After wandering in the desert for a long time, Moses finally came to a high, mountainous, country called Midian. One evening he came to a deep well with good clear water in it. He sat at the edge of the well to rest and while he was there, seven girls came with their sheep. They lifted the water out of the well with jugs and poured it into a large stone basin for their sheep.

Suddenly some men came along with more sheep. They rudely chased the girls away. 'Get out of our way,' they said. 'Our sheep must drink first. You'll have to wait until we're finished.'

The girls were afraid of the men, so they quickly made room for them at the well. But Moses wasn't afraid. When he saw how mean the men were to the girls, he became very angry. Standing in front of the newcomers, he said, 'These girls were here first and they must give their sheep water first. Don't you dare bother them again!'

Moses called the girls back and helped them with their sheep. Soon the animals were watered and the girls went happily on their way home because they had finished their work so early. The seven girls were sisters and their father was a priest, an old servant of God. 'My, you're home early tonight,' said the father.

The girls told their father about the man who had helped them at the well.

'And where is the man now?' asked the father.

'Why, he must still be sitting at the well,' answered the girls.

'Shame on you. Hurry and ask this kind man to come and have supper with us tonight.'

So Moses came into the home of the old priest and stayed overnight.

Later they asked him to live with them like one of the family. After a while he married one of the seven sisters, whose name was Zipporah.

Moses now had a home and a wife to share his life with. He had to earn a living so he helped with the sheep. Each day he would go into the fields with the sheep to find rich green grass for them. Each evening he would bring them to the well to let them drink. Whenever wild animals came to hurt the sheep, Moses would chase them away. How Moses had changed! Once he had been a wealthy prince but now he was a poor shepherd. Once his life had been easy but now he had to work hard each day, looking after sheep. He used to be quick-tempered and hot-headed, because he had wanted to help his people, but now he was learning to be patient.

Moses waited a long time for God to help the people of Israel. For forty years he worked as a shepherd, tending the family sheep and nothing happened. He hardly thought about his people any more. In fact, he had almost forgotten them as he grew older. But God hadn't forgotten the people of Israel.

One day as Moses walked in the field with the sheep he saw a very strange thing happening. A large bush was burning. This wasn't a very unusual thing in the desert, as there were fires from time to time, but this particular bush didn't seem to be burning up. Although there were flames, the leaves and branches on the bush remained as green as ever.

'I must take a closer look,' thought Moses, 'for this is a miracle!' As he walked closer, he heard a voice come out of the flames. 'Moses, Moses!' called the voice.

Moses was surprised and frightened. He answered, 'Here I am...!' And the voice said, 'You may not come any closer, Moses, for I am here. I am the God of Abraham, Isaac, and Jacob.'

Hearing this, Moses fell on his knees and listened to what the Lord had to tell him. He didn't dare look up while God told him he now wanted to help the people of Israel. The Lord wanted to bring them to the Promised Land. Moses was to go to the king of Egypt and tell him he must let the Israelites go.

Moses had changed a lot in the forty years he had tended sheep. Once Moses had dared to do all kinds of things but now he didn't care to go to the king at all! Moses would much prefer God to send another man to Egypt and leave him alone to remain a shepherd. But the Lord told Moses he had to go, and he didn't dare say, 'No' to God.

The Lord told Moses he would help and protect him and told him to take his brother Aaron along with him. Suddenly everything grew quiet again. The voice no longer spoke and the bush didn't burn any more. It was as though nothing had happened! Moses brought his sheep to their fold and went home. Someone else would have to care for them now because he could no longer do it himself. The Lord had given him other work to do. He would be allowed to help bring his people to the Promised Land. Moses then started on the long trip back to Egypt. Now he was no longer afraid for he knew God would watch over him.

Moses returns to Egypt

Read: Exodus 4–12

Moses' return to Egypt was a long tiring journey. On the way, a man as old as Moses came out to meet him. It was his brother, Aaron. Moses was so happy to see his brother again after all these years that he threw his arms round him and kissed him. Then he told him all that the Lord had said from the burning bush as they made their way towards Egypt.

First they went to the people of Israel and told them the Lord was going to set them free to live in a land he had promised to them. The heavy work and all the cruel punishment would soon be over. They were very happy and thanked God.

Moses and Aaron then went to the king who lived in a beautiful palace. He sat on a golden chair in a magnificent room looking very proud, and around him were many servants. Moses and Aaron were not afraid. They knew the Lord was watching over them as they stood before the king. They said, 'The Lord, the God of Israel says: "Let my people go out of Egypt".'

The king was angry and said, 'No, the people of Israel must stay here, to work for me.'

'But the Lord himself has said it,' replied Moses and Aaron. 'Surely you have to obey God.'

The king became furious and shouted, 'I don't know the Lord, and I don't want to obey him, either! I'll have nothing to do with your God. I'm the ruler over these people and will continue to be so. From now on I'll make them work harder than ever, and if they don't finish their work, I'll have them beaten twice as hard. Go away and get on with your own work.'

So they left, but they were very sad, for everything was now even worse. Surely, if the Lord were not with Moses and Aaron, the people would never be able to leave Egypt! But Moses and Aaron were not alone, for God was with them. He would see to it that the king would obey his orders. The Lord would punish him for his disobedience by sending ten terrible plagues to the king and the Egyptian people.

First of all the water in Egypt changed to blood so that the people had nothing to drink. After that a great many frogs were everywhere, skipping and hopping all around. They were in all the rooms of the Egyptians' houses and even jumped into the food and onto the people's beds.

The king became frightened so he called Moses and Aaron and said, 'I will let the people go, but first you must take these awful frogs away.'

Moses was glad, and he prayed to the Lord. All the frogs died and the plague was over, but as soon as the king saw this, he was no longer afraid. He said, 'I promised I would let the people go, but I have changed my mind. All the people must remain here.'

Then another punishment came. The dust on the earth changed to lice which bit the Egyptians.

In addition to the lice, swarms of flies came to bother the people. There was no place to hide from the pests. Again the king promised to let the people of Israel go but, as soon as the plague was gone, he went back on his word.

The plagues became worse. All the animals in Egypt grew sick. The cows and the sheep died, but the animals of the Israelites remained healthy. The people of Egypt themselves grew ill with big painful boils all over their bodies. Then there was a big hailstorm. The wheat was beaten to the ground, leaves were torn from the trees and the people caught in the hailstorm were killed. Yet the king still wouldn't obey.

Locusts came! They were only small insects but they came in swarms like huge clouds. There were so many locusts in the air it grew dark in the middle of the day. Everywhere the locusts landed they would eat all the grass and leaves. They ate and ate until all the crops in the fields disappeared. Still the king wouldn't obey!

Then it grew so dark one couldn't see a thing. Even though it was the middle of the day, the sun didn't shine. It was just like night and it lasted three days. The people sat huddled close together in their houses, very afraid. Even the king in his palace was afraid but still he wouldn't obey God!

Then came the last plague, which was the most terrible of all. It was evening and the people of Egypt were going to bed. They had no idea what was about to happen. That particular evening, however, the people of Israel were not getting ready for bed. They were all dressed and ready to leave, with all the things they wanted to take with them packed in preparation. The Lord had told Moses that the people would start their long journey to Canaan that very night.

First the Israelites must eat their last meal in Egypt. Each family baked bread and prepared a fresh lamb. The bread and the lambs were placed on the tables. It was to be a great feast for Israel, for that night they were to become free people. Each father took the lamb's blood outside, and with brushes made from leaves, they painted the blood on the doorposts. They put the blood on the left and on the right side and also above the door. In each home of the Israelites they did the same thing until every door became red with blood. Then night fell.

During this last night came the final terrible punishment. An angel came down from heaven and went through the streets into every Egyptian home and wherever he went, the oldest son died in his sleep. Even the king's house was not passed by.

But when the angel came to the houses of the people of Israel he didn't go in. Whenever he came to a door marked with the blood of a lamb he passed by the house. The Lord had told the angel that when he saw blood on the door, he must not go in. The sign of the blood saved the people of Israel. That night the people of Israel celebrated.

The Egyptians, however, were not celebrating, for they were terribly sad because a son had died in every home. Everyone was afraid and the king had no choice but to let the people of Israel go. 'Let those people go!' he shouted.

The Egyptians went to the people of Israel and gave them all kinds of beautiful things made of gold and silver. 'Here,' they said. 'You may have all these things but you must go away quickly!'

When morning came, the people of Israel started their long journey with their children, their animals and all the gifts from the frightened Egyptians. At last they were on their way to the promised land of Canaan.

Israelites led through the Sea

Read: Exodus 13 and 14

The journey to Canaan was a long one, and the people of Israel would have to walk all the way. There were many children and animals so they had to travel very slowly. Never before had the people of Israel been so far away from Egypt. They hadn't any idea where they were going. They knew of course, that they were on their way to the Promised Land, but they didn't know how to get there. So they followed Moses as he led the way with God's help.

In the blue sky a white cloud floated ahead of the Israelites. This was the cloud of the Lord and it showed them the way. God himself was travelling with them into this strange land. The Lord took good care of his people. He guided them through the desert with a pillar of cloud during the day. In the evenings, when the sun set, it did not grow dark, for there was a flame in the cloud, which gave some light. God promised to lead and protect them.

After three days of travelling, the people of Israel came to the sea. As they neared the shore they heard a great noise behind them, and when they turned they saw clouds of dust as horses and chariots thundered towards them. The Egyptians were coming after them; the king had changed his mind again. The king was sorry he had allowed the Israelites to leave his country and he was coming with his soldiers to force them back to Egypt. The people were terrified for they could go no further. In front of them was the sea and behind them were well-armed soldiers. They cried and wailed in fear.

Moses shouted, 'Don't be afraid! The Lord is with us. Come along and follow me. You won't have to fight the soldiers because the Lord will fight for you. Just be quiet and come along.'

When the people heard this, they did as they were told and followed Moses towards the sea. The water was very deep and the waves roared against the shore but Moses lifted his staff high above the water. The Lord sent a wind that blew the water aside.

Soon a path of dry land was formed right through the sea, with the water on either side like a great wall. Moses walked straight between the walls of water. Behind him marched all the people of Israel. The cloud followed behind the people, between them and the soldiers. It meant, 'Don't be afraid, I am watching over you.' On the side of the people of Israel, the cloud gave light, but on the side facing the Egyptian soldiers, it was dark.

Just then the king and his soldiers reached the sea. They looked to see where the Israelites had gone. Then they saw them in the middle of the sea between the walls of water. The king and his soldiers were so angry they didn't stop to think what a great miracle it was. 'Forward!' shouted the king. 'We'll get them yet! We'll show them!'

The king rode into the sea on his chariot followed by his soldiers. They rode as fast as they could trying to catch up with the Israelites, but they couldn't see in the darkness of the cloud that passed in front of them.

When morning came the people of Israel had reached the other side of the sea, but the Egyptians were still in the middle. The Lord said to Moses, 'Now stretch out your hand over the water.'

Moses stretched out his hand and the water flowed back over the path of the Egyptians, covering the horses and chariots of the king and his soldiers until they all drowned.

The king and his soldiers had done terrible things to the people of Israel but they would never harm them again.

At last the people of Israel were free. They celebrated by the side of the sea and sang to thank the Lord:

'Sing to the Lord, for he is highly exalted. The horse and the rider he has thrown into the sea.'

Israelites led through the Desert

Read: Exodus 15–17

The people of Israel had walked safely through the middle of the Red Sea, but the king and all his soldiers died when the waters closed over them. Now the people were free and they could travel on in peace to the Promised Land. The people would not lose their way through the strange countryside because the Lord would show them where to go.

Sometimes the Israelites forgot God's promise. After a short while they began to grumble when everything didn't run as smoothly as they thought it should. When things didn't go well they became afraid and forgot that the Lord was with them.

The Israelites came to a desert which they had to cross. There was nothing but sand and stones and it was very hot. The older people and children grew thirsty from walking over the hot sand, but there were no wells or streams from which to get water.

One day they came across a pool of water but it was so bitter they couldn't drink it. The Israelites began to grumble and complain to Moses. 'What are we going to drink now?'

Moses quietly took a piece of wood and threw it into the water, as the Lord had told him to do. 'Now drink!' he said. 'The water is all right now.'

Sure enough, the bitter water had suddenly become fresh and sweet. Of course the wood alone hadn't done this, nor had Moses. Only the Lord has the power to do such a thing. Surely the Israelites would now believe God's promise to look after them?

A few days later all the bread and meat they had taken out of Egypt was finished. When they had nothing left to eat they began to grumble again. 'In Egypt we had enough food to eat so why didn't you leave us there? Why did you take us away to let us die of hunger here in the desert?'

Moses told them not to grumble. 'The Lord will take care of you. Tonight he is going to give you meat and tomorrow he will send bread from heaven. Then will you believe that he cares for you?'

That evening a huge flock of birds came flying towards them. They were big fat birds called quail. They were so tired of flying that they fell to the ground between the tents where the Israelites were camping. They picked up the birds and cooked them over their fires. They had as much meat as they wanted.

The next morning, when the people went outside, the ground was white, as if it had snowed overnight. There were countless tiny round white flakes. 'What is it?' asked the people.

'It is manna,' Moses explained. 'Bread which the Lord has given us to eat.'

The people gathered it as fast as they could, scooping up handfuls and jugfuls - as much as they could eat. They were able to eat it raw, bake it into cakes or cook it as a sort of porridge. It tasted good and each morning there was plenty for the people to gather. Now they knew that they would never again have to suffer hunger, and were sure the Lord would take care of all their needs. Surely they would now learn to trust in God. Sadly, however, their faith was very weak. Once again, when they ran out of water they were very angry with Moses and blamed him for it.

'Lord, what shall I do?' he prayed.

The Lord told Moses to go to a large rock which was enclosed by the camp and strike it with his staff. With all the people following him, shouting and complaining,

Moses did as the Lord had said and the stone split open. A stream of cold water flowed out and the people were quiet as they rushed over to quench their thirst.

Later another wonderful thing happened. The Israelites could surely tell that God was watching over his people. A large band of thieves who lived in the desert came to steal and rob from them. Moses realised that he would have to do something about it. He called on Joshua, a young man who was a good fighter but who, more importantly, loved the Lord.

'This can't go on any longer. Pick out the strongest of our men to fight the robbers and give them such a beating that they'll never dare to come back again.'

When Joshua and his men went out to fight the thieves, Moses climbed a nearby hill to watch the battle and to pray to the Lord to help them. Stretching out his hands towards heaven, he called, 'Lord, please help us!' As he continued to pray, keeping his hands held up high, the Lord heard him and the Israelites defeated the enemy. Once again, God had blessed them and had answered their prayers.

The Golden Calf

Read: Exodus 19–32

The people of Israel travelled on, with the white cloud ahead of them to show the way. They reached the country where Moses had lived for a long time as a shepherd and the cloud stopped above a high mountain called Sinai. When they came to the foot of the mountain the Israelites decided to stay there for a while. The Lord had told them that he was going to meet them there and that something special would happen.

Everyone put on their best clothes and early in the morning of that special day, they stood waiting close to the mountain. As the cloud hung over the summit they heard the sound of thunder and the whole mountain began to shake and tremble. Then it became very quiet and all the people heard the voice of God speaking to them.

He told them that they must always obey him, love him above all others, and love one another also. God gave ten commandments by which they should lead their lives. Provided they obeyed the Lord they would be blessed, and would be the happiest people in the world.

Later, the thunder started again and everyone ran back to their tents, for they were afraid to stay too close to the mountain. This time Moses climbed to the top of Sinai to write down everything the Lord said, so that the Israelites would never forget his words. The people watched him go higher and higher until finally he disappeared into the cloud on the summit.

That evening they waited for Moses to return, but darkness fell and there was no sign of him. Neither did he appear the following day. When he had not come back after a further two days the people began to worry and said, 'Perhaps Moses will never return! Maybe he has had an accident and he is dead. Who will take us to Canaan if we have no one to lead us?'

Then some of them began to say, 'We cannot see God anyway, so perhaps he has left us too. Other nations have an image of their god, in front of which they kneel and pray, so why can't we? Let us make a golden image which we can carry with us to Canaan.'

So they went to Aaron, who was in charge while Moses was away. 'Make us a god we can see and carry to the Promised Land.'

Aaron was taken aback at their suggestion, but the crowd seemed angry and he was afraid of what they would do if he refused. So he told them to bring all the gold they had so that he could melt it down and mould it into an idol. The people did this and Aaron made a large golden calf similar to what they had seen in Egypt. Then the Israelites could kneel before it to pray.

The people were delighted and began to shout and dance for joy around the golden calf. The noise was so great that it could be heard on the top of Mount Sinai. As they were shouting and dancing, suddenly a man stepped into the centre of the crowd. It was Moses, back from the top of the mountain! He wasn't afraid of the people as Aaron had been and he was very angry with them. As the crowd watched, Moses took the golden calf, turned it upside down and then burned it on a blazing fire until there was nothing left of the idol. Then the people were worried when they realised how they had sinned against God. They began to wonder whether God would ever forgive them.

The next day Moses climbed the mountain again, but he was sad and afraid this time when he knelt before the Lord: 'Oh Lord, these people have done a great sin and deserve a terrible punishment, but please remain their friend. Let me take the punishment in their place.'

Despite what they had done, and although they had disobeyed the Lord, he still loved the children of Israel and wanted them to be his people. God loved them much more than Moses ever possibly could.

The Israelites doubt God again

Read: Numbers 13–14

The Israelites lived near the slopes of Mount Sinai for nearly a year before they continued on their way to Canaan. Each day they came a little closer to the Promised Land, until one day they were able to catch sight of the mountains of Canaan in the distance. Then the cloud stopped and they set up camp to rest for a few days before continuing into the new land.

Now, at that time, other people were living in Canaan who did not worship the God of Israel. Before Moses could lead his people into the Promised Land there were many things he had to find out. He wanted to know how many people lived there and how strong their armies were. Then he had to learn if there was good grazing and plenty of food to eat. Moses had to find out if the land was as wonderful as everyone hoped it would be.

Moses chose twelve brave and strong men to go into Canaan as spies. One was Joshua, whose army had defeated the robbers who attacked the Israelites. Moses told them, 'Climb those mountains and go into the land of Canaan. There you must have a good look at everything before coming back to tell us what you saw. Be careful that the Canaanites don't catch you!'

The next day the twelve men set out for the Promised Land. The Israelites waited impatiently for their return as they were eager to hear all about Canaan. After what seemed a long time, the twelve men came back to the camp, bringing with them many things to show the people. They carried all kinds of delicious fruit: pomegranates, juicy figs and large clusters of grapes which were so heavy two men had to carry them between them, tied to a stick over their shoulders. 'If Canaan has beautiful fruit like this,' said the Israelites, 'it must be a wonderful country!'

Joshua and Caleb, two of the twelve men who really loved the Lord, reported that it was a wonderful country and that they believed that God would lead them safely there. But the other ten didn't have faith in God. They said, 'There are flowers and fruit everywhere and plenty of grass for our cattle, but we cannot go into Canaan. The people who live there are far too strong for us. We even saw giants, so tall that we felt like puppets next to them. We will never be able to defeat them.'

The Israelites grew afraid when they heard the news. Once again they had forgotten the Lord who watched over them and the thought of the giants scared them even more. But Joshua and Caleb trusted the Lord and told the people, 'Don't be afraid! The Lord will help us for he has promised to give us that country and we believe he will. You must believe it too.'

But they didn't believe that God would lead them into Canaan. Instead they began to moan and complain, grumbling against God and Moses. 'If only we had stayed in Egypt. Why did God bring us here to let us be killed by giants? There is no way we will go into the land of Canaan. Let's go back to Egypt.'

Joshua and Caleb tried to reason with them but the people didn't pay any attention. They became so angry with Joshua and Caleb that they tried to kill them. They were on the point of stoning them to death when God stepped in to save them. A glaring white light came from the cloud like a bolt of lightning from heaven.

The crowd screamed in terror, covering their faces from the dazzling light and fell back shaking with fear.

'As a punishment for failing to trust the Lord,' Moses told them, 'He has said that you will not enter into Canaan but will wander in the desert until your children have grown up. Then they will enter the land of Canaan instead of you. All except Joshua and Caleb, who believed in the Lord, will die in the desert.'

Despite this warning some of them wanted to enter the Promised Land. The next morning they came to Moses and said, 'Yesterday we were disobedient and afraid but now we want to go into Canaan and will fight bravely against the people who live there.'

Moses shook his head sadly and told them, 'Don't go. God will not allow you to enter Canaan.'

The men decided to go anyway. Though they fought bravely the Lord didn't help them and they were all killed by the Canaanites. The others turned back and the cloud led the way again. But as they journeyed into the desert, further away from the Promised Land, their heads were bent down and their hearts were full of sadness.

Travelling through the Desert

Read: Numbers 20–21

The Israelites continued deeper into the desert until they had left Canaan far behind. It was a sad journey and they continued to grumble and complain. When they had difficulty finding water they blamed Moses and Aaron: 'Why did you bring us here? It's your fault we're so thirsty!' As he had done once before, God showed Moses a rock which would provide them with water. Shouting and grumbling, the people followed. Moses lost his temper:

'Listen, you disobedient people! Shall we let water gush out of this rock for you?' And he struck the rock hard twice in a fit of anger!

Water gushed out and everyone rushed forward to drink. Everyone was happy for a short time but Moses and Aaron regretted their quick temper for it was as if they had not believed that God would look after them. So God told Moses and Aaron, 'Because you have forgotten me, you may not enter the land of Canaan either.'

The manna which the Lord provided for them appeared every morning as before, but after a while the people began to complain about it: 'Manna, every day the same!' as they kicked it into the sand when they found it.

God was not pleased with their attitude and things got worse for them. One day poisonous snakes came crawling into the tents and bit the people. Many died, and when there was nothing that anyone could do about it everyone became afraid. They pleaded with Moses, 'Please help us. Pray to God for his forgiveness and please ask him to take away the horrible snakes.'

So Moses prayed and the Lord heard him. But instead of taking the snakes away, God worked a miracle. Moses gathered the people together. Holding a long stick on top of which was a snake made of bronze, he told them that if they were bitten, they were to look up at it and they wouldn't die. In this way God wanted to teach the people that they must always trust him and look to him for help. If they did so they would have nothing to fear.

Moses goes to be with God

Read: Deuteronomy 32–34

After many years of wandering through the desert their long journey was almost over and the people of Israel came close to the land of Canaan. Many of the older people had died and their children had grown up, but after all this time they wondered how they would actually get into the Promised Land. Would the Lord help them to defeat the people who were there?

The Promised Land lay ahead of the Israelites. In the distance they could see the mountains and it wouldn't be long before they could enter. But Moses couldn't go any further as God had told him that he would not go into Canaan because of his disobedience. His brother Aaron had already died. The Lord told Moses that he would only see the land from a distance and would not enter the land that he was giving to the Israelites.

Moses still loved the Lord for he remembered all the wonderful ways in which God had protected him from danger: from his birth in Egypt to that moment when he had finally shown the people the way to the land of Canaan. When Moses thought about all that the Lord had done for him he was happy again.

Moses wanted to speak to the people for one last time. He wanted them to remember that they must always be obedient to the Lord and remain close to him, for only then would they be happy in the new land. Moses told them what would happen if they forgot the Lord. They would be unhappy and wouldn't be allowed to remain in Canaan.

Then Moses said goodbye to the Israelites and walked away alone towards a nearby mountain. As the people watched, he climbed higher and higher until he disappeared out of sight.

When Moses reached the top of the mountain the Lord came to join him. Moses could see a great distance from the mountain top. He could see the fertile land where his people were soon to live, and God showed him the green pastures and the rivers which ran through them. He showed him the mountains, the trees and the sea beyond. Moses saw the whole country and knew that the people of Israel were going to be very happy there.

Then the Lord took him to be with himself in heaven, to a land far more beautiful than Canaan.

As both Aaron and Moses were no longer with the Israelites to lead them into the Promised Land, Joshua, the brave soldier, took charge. It was not to be an easy task for Joshua. He knew he would have to be very careful, for there were still many wicked people to be defeated in the land of Canaan before they could enter.

Rahab and the Scarlet Cord

Read: Joshua 2

The first place they had to conquer was Jericho, a city with a strong wall around it. Before Joshua could lead the people any further he had to find out about this city. How thick and strong were the walls and how many soldiers were there? So he called two men and told them, 'I want you to go to the land of Canaan. Go quietly and enter the city of Jericho. You must see everything you can and then come back to tell me all about it. The Lord will watch over you.'

Bravely they set out and soon reached Jericho. The wall was too high for them to climb over. Set in the wall was a large gate and people were going in and out. The two men mingled with the crowd and walked through the gate without anybody noticing them. Once inside the city they walked through the streets, looking at everything very carefully.

When evening came and it grew dark the two men had to find somewhere to sleep. They walked round the city along the top of the wall and came to a house built into it. When the men knocked at the door they met a woman called Rahab who was willing to give them a bed for the night.

Some of the men in the city had seen the two strangers go into Rahab's house and quickly ran to tell the king, who sent soldiers to arrest the spies. The soldiers banged on the door:

'Rahab, open the door! Where are the strangers? They are enemies, who have come to spy on our land and we have come to take them.'

What would Rahab do now? Should she let the soldiers in and hand the spies over to them? But Rahab had already hidden the men on top of the flat roof under some flax stalks. 'If you run fast,' she told the soldiers, 'you'll be able to catch up with them for they were here just a short while ago.'

The soldiers ran off to track down the Israelites. Then Rahab went to the roof and called to the two men. She knew very well who they were because she had heard of the people of Israel before. She also knew that God was with them and this was why she had offered to help them.

'The Lord will surely give you the city and all this country,' she said. 'Your God can do all things. We have heard how he brought your people through the middle of the sea and did many other great things. This is why the people here are so afraid of you and why I have been kind to you. Now I want you to promise me that you will be kind to me. In a little while you will come and take this city away from us. Will you remember me then and ensure no harm comes to me? Will you also remember my father and mother, my brothers and sisters?'

The men promised to protect them and told her to put a scarlet, red, cord outside her window so that the soldiers of Israel would know where she and her family lived. Then they hurried to get away in case the king's soldiers returned to find them in Rahab's house.

Rahab took them into the living-room and opened the window. Taking a strong red rope she let one end out over the wall and tied the other end to the window. The two men climbed down the rope and disappeared into the night. They hid in the mountains for a few days before returning safely back to Joshua. God had looked after them and made sure Rahab would shelter them, even though she did not know them.

Joshua and the Battle of Jericho

Read: Joshua 6

A few days later the Israelites marched towards the walls of the city of Jericho. The inhabitants saw them coming and quickly locked the gates. Then they went to the top of the wall and prepared to defend themselves. The wall was too thick and strong to be demolished and the gates could not be easily broken down. But the Israelites didn't even try to attack the city, much to the surprise of the soldiers on top of the wall.

The Israelites just walked around the city in a long parade. They walked around the city only once, then they left.

The next day they came again and walked once more around the city. For five days they did the same, walking once round the walls before going back to their camp. When the Israelites walked around the city on the sixth day the people of Jericho were very puzzled. They laughed about it and said, 'What do they think they are doing? Do they think they can take our city just by walking around it?'

But the Israelites were doing this because God had told Joshua to do it. When the seventh day came the people of Israel came out once again, but this time they kept on marching until they had gone round Jericho seven times. Then they stood still. Suddenly they started to shout and cheer.

As they cheered, the wall began to crack and crumble until, with a huge crash, all the stones came tumbling down! With no wall to block their way, the Israelites were able to walk straight into the city and capture it. No one in Jericho was left alive except for Rahab's family whom God had promised to protect. The one part of the wall left standing was a house with a length of red rope hanging from a window. It was the house of Rahab who had helped the two spies. She was saved with her family and they joined the people of Israel. The Israelites then went much further into Canaan and drove the people out.

After all the cities had been taken they set up home in the Promised Land. They built houses for themselves, sowed grain on their farms and put cattle and sheep out to graze in the fresh green pastures of Canaan. Now they had everything they could possibly want. No longer did they have to suffer thirst, for there was plenty of fresh water and good milk. No longer did they need manna, for now they could make their own bread from wheat which they grew; and there was lots of delicious fruit and honey.

Joshua told the Israelites, 'You must always remember that it was the Lord who gave you this land. The people who lived here before used to pray to idols and you must never do this. You must pray to God and love him always. You must obey him and do all that he asks.'

'Yes, we will always do this! The Lord is our God!' they replied.

Gideon and the Sword of the Lord

Read: Judges 6–7

It was summer and the grain had ripened on the farms. Everywhere people were harvesting their crops. They would thresh their grain and grind it into flour to make bread. However, there was some concern because, for a few years, when the wheat was ripe, robbers came to steal it and many people were left without bread.

When the farmers were gathering their crops they had to watch to see if anyone was coming to rob them. A young man called Gideon gathered his crop one day. Then he pounded the grain to make flour and quickly put it into sacks. He had to hide it in a safe place where the robbers wouldn't find it.

Gideon loved the Lord and he was pleased that he had been able to look after his grain. But he was sad that the Israelites had once more forgotten about God. The Israelites hadn't loved the Lord or obeyed his wishes. They had prayed to an idol, just like the people who lived there before and now thieves came to bother them every year. God sent the thieves to punish them! So Gideon prayed: 'Please Lord, chase the thieves away!'

As Gideon prayed he suddenly realised that he was no longer alone. He looked round and saw a man sitting on a rock under a tree. It was an angel who had come to give Gideon a message. The angel said that God had heard the people crying for help. 'When the robbers come again you must chase them away!'

Gideon couldn't believe what he had heard. 'How can I do this? I am so young and the robbers are so strong!'

But the angel answered, 'You can do it, Gideon! The Lord is going to help you.' When Gideon heard this, he felt better. He knew that the Lord would help him to do what was asked of him.

But Gideon wanted to be certain before he attacked the robbers. He wanted God to give him a sign. He took a sheepskin, which was like a thick blanket, and put it on the grass. Then he prayed, 'Dear Lord, every morning the grass is wet with dew. Tomorrow morning, however, allow the grass to be dry and the blanket wet. Then I shall know you will help me.'

The next morning it was exactly as he had asked. The grass was dry and the blanket soaking wet. Gideon could wring out a whole bowlful of water. Although Gideon believed the Lord would help him he wanted one more sign. 'This time, Lord, let the grass be wet and the blanket dry.' The next morning he found the blanket was dry and the grass wet with dew. Now Gideon was in no doubt that the Lord would help him to defeat the thieves.

Calling an army together he led them straight to the robbers' camp, but God told them that his army was too big! So Gideon sent most of his men home, just as God had told him. Now there was only a small company left. But Gideon wasn't afraid, for the Lord had told him he would help. To Gideon's surprise God said, 'You still have too many men. Send more away.' Gideon did as he was told. Now there was only a very small group. Could this little band fight against such a large number of the enemy?

Night fell. It was dark and quiet and the thieves were fast asleep in their tents. Gideon and his men crept up to the camp and suddenly began to blow loudly on their trumpets, shattering the quiet of the night! Gideon's men also smashed bottles on the ground making an even greater noise. Each man carried a wooden torch, which they swung round and round. It was a very strange sight indeed. Then they all shouted, 'The sword of the Lord and of Gideon!' as they ran down towards the robbers' tents as fast as they could.

The thieves were frightened. All they could see was the circle of advancing light which they believed was an army much stronger than they were. Back and forth they ran, bumping into each other in fright, terrified of the Israelites and of each other. Not daring to remain in their camp for another minute, they ran for their lives, with Gideon's men chasing after them until they left the country altogether. They did not return. The Israelites were overjoyed and they all came to thank Gideon. But Gideon told them, 'You mustn't thank me, you must thank the Lord! He answered our prayers and set us free.'

Ruth and Naomi

Read: Ruth 1–4

In the town of Bethlehem, in the land of Canaan, there was a woman called Naomi who lived with her husband and two sons. One year a drought came to the land and all the plants shrivelled and died leaving Naomi with no grain to grind and no flour to make bread. The family had nothing to eat. Naomi's neighbours were unable to help as they had no grain either. It was the same all over the country.

So Naomi, her husband and two sons decided to move to another country called Moab, where there was plenty of wheat and nobody was hungry. For many years Naomi lived in Moab but a great deal of sadness came into her life. First her husband died. Her two sons married girls from Moab, one called Ruth and the other Orpah. Sadly her two sons also fell ill and died. She became a sad, lonely woman. 'I don't want to stay here any longer,' she said. 'It is better for me to return to my own country, where there is surely enough bread for me to eat by now.'

So Naomi set out to return to Bethlehem in Canaan. The two girls, Ruth and Orpah, kept her company part of the way, because they loved Naomi very dearly and were sorry that she was leaving Moab. She had been a kind and loving mother-in-law to them and she had told them about the God of Israel.

When they had travelled some distance, Naomi said, 'This is far enough. You should turn back now. You have both been kind to me and I hope the Lord will bless you and make you happy.'

First, Orpah kissed Naomi and, as she bade farewell, there were tears running down her cheeks. She was sorry to leave Naomi, but she wanted to return to be with her own people in Moab.

Ruth also wept but she didn't want to go back. She loved Naomi too much and decided to stay with her, live in Bethlehem and worship the God of Israel. With the Israelites, Ruth felt she could serve the Lord.

'No, I can never leave you! Your people are my people, your God is my God. I want to remain with you always.'

Naomi was very pleased to have Ruth with her and so they travelled on to Bethlehem together. When they arrived the people saw a great change in Naomi. She had left as a young woman and had returned old and grey. They spoke about the sad old woman who had come back from Moab after so many years, and talked about Ruth who didn't want to leave Naomi to live on her own.

As it was summer, there was plenty of wheat and everyone was busily harvesting the crops. But poor Naomi hadn't any wheat as nothing had been planted on her land. Without wheat there would be no flour, and without flour there could be no bread.

Ruth offered to look for some leftover wheat on the farms where the men were harvesting. Ruth went to the men working in the field: 'May I pick up the ears of grain which you drop along the way?'

It was common practice for the men to allow the poor to follow behind and pick up any grain which had dropped, so they told Ruth it was all right. She looked carefully all morning and by lunch-time she had gathered quite a lot. The men to whom Ruth had spoken were the servants of a wealthy gentleman called Boaz. When he came to see how the work was coming along on his farm he saw the young girl looking for grain, he asked, 'Who is that girl?'

'That is Ruth,' his servants told him, 'who came from the land of Moab with old Naomi.'

Boaz had heard many kind things about Ruth and he was glad she had come to his farm. Walking over to her, he said, 'You may come here for wheat every day. I will ask my servants to be kind to you and when you are thirsty they will give you a drink. You don't have to go to any other farms.'

Ruth was very happy indeed. Bowing low before the kind gentleman, she asked, 'Why are you taking such good care of me?'

'Because you have been kind to Naomi,' answered Boaz.

At noon the tired men went to eat their lunch and Boaz said to Ruth, 'Come along! You may eat with us.'

He gave Ruth delicious bread and sweet wine to satisfy her thirst. Later, when lunch was finished, Ruth went on looking for wheat. Boaz whispered to his servants, 'You must see to it that Ruth finds plenty of wheat. Drop a few extra ears here and there so that she can pick them up.'

Needless to say, Ruth found a lot of wheat that day. When evening came, she threshed the ears of grain and came home with a big bag of wheat kernels. Naomi was pleased and surprised. 'Where did you go to get all this?' she asked. Ruth told her everything that had happened.

The next day she went out again to the farm of Boaz and again the day after that. Ruth continued to gather wheat on Boaz' farm for as long as the men were harvesting. One day, after all the grain had been harvested, Boaz asked Ruth to marry him. So Ruth, who had been poor, became the wife of a wealthy farmer and some time later they had a little son. Naomi was delighted too: 'I have had great sadness in my life, but the Lord has made everything right again.'

Samuel, Servant of God

Read: 1 Samuel 1–4

There once lived a woman called Hannah who was very unhappy because she was unable to have children. To make matters worse, her husband's other wife, Peninnah teased her. 'The Lord has forgotten you and doesn't love you, that's why he doesn't give you a child!' Whenever Hannah thought about this, tears came to her eyes. However, each year Hannah travelled to Jerusalem with her husband to visit the tabernacle, the house of God. There they would bring an offering to the Lord and pray and Hannah would receive a gift from her husband because he loved her very much.

Although he wanted to make her happy she knew that only the Lord could make her really happy by answering her prayer.

One year when they were visiting the tabernacle Peninnah teased Hannah so much that Hannah couldn't eat. 'I will tell the Lord about my grief,' she said. When she came to the tabernacle she went inside and fell on her knees to pray. 'Dear God, please listen to me. Please don't forget me. Give me a child and I will take good care of him. I will tell him about you every day and I will do everything I can to help him to be your servant.'

Hannah prayed for a long time. She didn't want anyone to hear her so she whispered very softly. Nearby, at the door of the tabernacle, sat Eli, the high priest. He was God's servant and head over all the other priests. It was his job to look after the tabernacle. Eli saw Hannah and thought, 'This woman is acting strangely. She just lies there on the ground with her lips moving, but I don't hear her voice. Perhaps she's drunk.' He walked over and gruffly asked her, 'Aren't you ashamed to come to the house of God when you're drunk?'

Hannah's eyes were full of tears as she looked at Eli. 'Oh no, I'm not drunk! But I have been very sad and have been telling the Lord all about my grief. I have been praying to God.'

Eli was sorry he had been angry with her and said, 'Go in peace. The Lord has heard your prayer and He will answer you.'

When Hannah returned to her husband her sadness had gone. She believed with all her heart that the Lord had heard her prayer. Indeed, the Lord gave her the very thing for which she had asked. A year later Hannah had a baby boy and she called him Samuel, which means: 'I asked the Lord for him'. That year Hannah couldn't travel to the tabernacle with her husband because she had to stay at home to look after the baby.

A few years later she made the journey to the tabernacle and brought Samuel along too. He had grown into a fine sturdy boy who no longer needed his mother every day. Now he could become God's servant in the tabernacle. Together Samuel and Hannah went to speak to Eli, who was sitting by the door. He had grown much older and his hair was almost white. He didn't recognise Hannah, so she introduced herself: 'I am the woman who prayed here for a baby. This is the boy who was given to me by the Lord, and I promised him that he would be his servant. May he remain here in the tabernacle and help you?'

Eli was very glad to have Samuel to work in the temple for him. Hannah returned home alone but she was very happy that her son could remain in the house of God. Each year after this, she and her husband returned to see Samuel, and to give him a new robe to wear. Samuel was pleased to be a servant of God and he did all kinds of tasks for Eli.

One night Samuel woke up with a start when he heard someone calling him. He got up and went to the room where Eli was sleeping. 'Here I am,' he said, 'you called me, didn't you?'

But Eli answered, 'No, I didn't call you. Hurry back to bed!'

'Perhaps I was dreaming', thought Samuel and he went back to his room to sleep.

But he was wakened again: 'Samuel, Samuel!' a voice called. This time Samuel was sure he wasn't mistaken, so he went back to Eli's room and said, 'Here I am. Now you called me.'

But again Eli said, 'No, Samuel, I didn't call you. You must have dreamt it. Just go back to bed and sleep.'

Poor Samuel couldn't understand it at all, but he obeyed Eli and went back to his room.

He had just lain down when he heard the voice for the third time: 'Samuel, Samuel!' Back he went again to Eli: 'Surely you called me this time, didn't you?'

Then Eli realised whose voice it must be so he said, 'It was the Lord who called you. Go back and when you hear the voice again, say, "Speak Lord, your servant is listening.'

Samuel went back to his room where he lay quietly and waited. His heart thumped with reverence and fear. Did the Lord really want to speak to him? Again the voice of God spoke to him: 'Samuel, Samuel!'

Softly Samuel replied, 'Speak, Lord, for your servant is listening.'

Then the Lord spoke to Samuel. But the message from God was a very sad one. It was about the sons of Eli who did not love the Lord and who did not do what God had told them. God had warned them many times but they wouldn't listen.

Now the Lord was going to punish them. On hearing this, Samuel couldn't get back to sleep.

Early in the morning as usual, he rose and went outside to open the doors of the tabernacle. Eli called him and asked, 'What did the Lord tell you last night?'

Samuel had no choice but to tell him everything, even though the message was a very sad one for Eli and his family. Eli was stunned but simply said, 'He is the Lord. He must do what he thinks best.'

What God had said took place many years later when Samuel had grown up. War broke out and the men of Israel went to fight. Hophni and Phinehas, Eli's sons, were in the army and they were both killed on the same day. When their father heard the sad news he fell from his chair and also died.

Samuel was now the servant of God and he loved the Lord. Often he heard the voice of God speaking to him and he did everything the Lord told him to do.

David, the Shepherd

Read: 1 Samuel 16

Young David looked after his father's sheep. Early each morning he would go to the pen where the sheep sheltered for the night and each day he would take them to the fields. He was their shepherd and his job was to make sure they had enough to eat. When they were thirsty he would bring water for them to drink. He looked after them well. David also had to watch out for wild animals which might want to kill the sheep. When he saw one he would chase it away with stones from his sling or hit it with his shepherd's crook.

In the distance were the houses of Bethlehem where David's father and brothers lived. He was often alone in the fields with his sheep but he didn't mind at all as he was happy and content with life. To amuse himself he played on his harp and sang songs. The sound of his beautiful singing could be heard across the pastures.

David always felt as though there was somebody with him at all times. David loved the Lord and knew that God was everywhere. David thought, 'I'm taking care of the sheep and the Lord is taking care of me. The Lord is also a shepherd and I am one of his sheep.'

One day David was in the pasture with his flock when a lion came to kill a sheep. It crept through the bushes until suddenly it jumped on one of the sheep. When the lion pounced, David saw it and ran after it, not thinking about the danger to himself. When he caught up with the creature he struck out at it until it let go of the sheep. Then he killed the huge animal to make sure that it would not come back again to bother his sheep. Gently, David took the sheep back to the flock.

One day a servant came to tell David he must come home at once, as someone had come to visit his father, Jesse. David was the youngest of eight sons who all lived with their father. An old man with a long grey beard had come to the house. It was Samuel, who was now quite old, but still a good servant of God. The Lord had told him to go to the home of Jesse as one of his sons would one day become king of Israel.

There already was a king, called Saul, but he wasn't a very good ruler. He had become disobedient and no longer wanted to listen to God. Samuel didn't know which of the sons was to be the one chosen to follow Saul, but he knew that God would point him out when all the boys came before him.

First came the eldest. He was a big strong man and Samuel thought, 'Probably it's this one! What a handsome king he would be!'

'No, Samuel,' said the Lord. 'It isn't this one. I don't look to see if my king will be big and strong. I look into his heart.'

Samuel shook his head and said, 'No, the Lord didn't choose this one.'

The second son came next and again Samuel shook his head.

One by one, the sons of Jesse came to Samuel, but each time the old servant of God said, 'No, the Lord didn't choose this one.'

Finally, Samuel asked, 'Are these all the sons you have, Jesse?'

'No, the youngest isn't here. He is with the sheep in the pasture.'

'Send for him at once,' said Samuel.

And that was why David had been called home. Samuel was waiting for him as his father led him inside. Then the Lord told Samuel, 'This is the one. David must be king over my people for he loves me with all his heart.'

Samuel rose and took a horn out of his pocket. It was filled with special oil for anointing. Pouring out the sweet-smelling oil on David's head, he said, 'The Lord says, "I anoint you, David, as King of Israel. In a few years you will become king, for your heart is full of love for God."'

What an amazing message this was. David, only a humble shepherd boy, being anointed king of all the people of Israel. David believed what the Lord had said for, when God makes a promise, he always keeps his word. David and his father were very happy indeed. They didn't talk about it, however, and they didn't tell anyone what had happened, in case King Saul got to know about it. Saul assumed that his son Jonathan would become king after him; certainly not a shepherd boy from Bethlehem!

David goes to King Saul

Read: 1 Samuel 16

King Saul was in his palace. Around him were many servants who did everything he commanded them to do. He was very rich and powerful and could have anything he asked for. Despite this, the king was both angry and sad. Samuel, the servant of God, had told him he wouldn't be king much longer because he hadn't loved the Lord, nor had he wanted to obey him.

'Another man will become king,' Samuel told him. 'A man the Lord himself has chosen, who loves the Lord with all his heart. He will be king in your place. He will live in your palace and sit on your throne.'

King Saul thought about this all the time and was annoyed about it.

'I want to be king for as long as I live' he thought, 'and after I die, my son Jonathan must rule in my place! I wish I knew who this other man is, for I would kill him if I could.'

The more he thought about it, the angrier he became and sometimes he was so furious the servants were afraid of him.

They said to each other, 'Our king is sick. He is sick because God has left him and now his heart is dark and full of evil. I wish we could do something for him.'

Then they had an idea and went to see the king: 'Our lord, the King, we think it would help if somebody could come and play beautiful music for you. Perhaps it would be good for you and help you to get well again.'

'All right, go and find a man who can do this,' said the king.

One of the servants said, 'I know a shepherd in Bethlehem. He is the son of Jesse and can play wonderful music on his harp.'

'Very well,' said the king. 'Send for him.'

One of the servants then went to Bethlehem and brought David to the palace. The king was having one of his wild fits of temper when David arrived. He was stomping through the rooms, shouting with grief and fury.

As soon as David came in, he began to play one of his lovely songs. It was a beautiful tune and it was soothing to Saul's troubled mind.

When he listened, his anger slowly melted away and he no longer shouted or stomped around. The soft music seemed to take all his troubles away.

David's music helped the king to become well again, and he was very pleased for him to stay on in the palace to play regularly for him.

Saul grew very fond of David. Of course, Saul didn't know that the young man was the anointed king who would one day take his place.

David and Goliath

Read: 1 Samuel 17 and 18:1-4

War broke out in Israel when they were attacked by the Philistines, who came to steal sheep and grain from the people. King Saul called all his soldiers together to defend the country. The Philistines had a strong army and one man in particular was stronger than all the others. He was a giant of a man called Goliath. He carried a large spear in his hand and a big sword hung from the belt around his waist. He had a coat made of bright shining armour and on his head he wore a helmet which glinted in the sunlight.

Every day the giant would taunt the Israelites. 'Who wants to fight? I am stronger than all of you put together! Come here, if any of you dare!' He laughed at them and he cursed. He teased Saul and his soldiers but, worst of all, he mocked God.

Each day he came out but nobody dared to fight him. Three of David's brothers, big strong soldiers, were there, but none of them came forward. They were all afraid of the giant and they trembled with fear when they saw him coming.

David, meanwhile, had gone back home to his father. The king no longer had time to listen to music and David had returned home to look after the sheep.

One evening, Jesse called David and said, 'David, I want you to go to your brothers who are with Saul's army. Find out if they are all right and take them some food.' David was pleased to have the opportunity to go and see something of the war.

Early the next morning he set out on the long journey until he came to where the Israelites were. Just when he arrived Goliath came out again. He stood close to Saul's army, cursing and swearing, and mocking the soldiers. David was shocked when he heard it. The godless giant was mocking the king and insulting the Lord! David loved God with all his heart and this mockery made him very angry. Was there nobody to punish this wicked man?

When he learned that no one was brave enough to fight Goliath David said, 'I will fight him.'

'Do you really dare?' asked the soldiers. 'Do you really think you can fight this giant? If you do and win, you will receive the king's daughter for your wife and you will be given many fine presents. The king himself has said this.'

The soldiers brought David to the king. 'You are only a young shepherd boy,' said the king. 'How can you possibly want to fight with that giant? He is a big soldier, much bigger and stronger than you. No, I won't let you fight him.'

'The Lord will help me, O King!' said David. 'This is why I can fight the giant. Once I fought a lion while I was tending sheep and killed it, because the Lord helped me. I shall kill this wicked man who mocks God. The Lord will help me to fight the giant.'

The king listened and agreed only when he realised that no one else would fight. He ordered a servant to bring David a coat made of iron. He put the coat on David and placed a shiny helmet on his head. Then Saul gave him his own big sword. But all these things were much too heavy for David. Quickly he took the armour off and gave the sword back to Saul.

Instead of weapons and armour, David took only a stick and sling and he looked for five round smooth stones and put them in his pocket.

Then he went out to where the giant stood. When Goliath saw him coming he laughed and cursed!

'Who is this?' he bellowed. 'What kind of a little fellow are you? You don't even have a sword, just a stick! Do you think I am a dog? Do you believe you can chase me away with your stick? Come here and I will beat you to death. The wild animals will eat you up when I'm finished with you.'

Goliath was furious and all those who heard him trembled with fear. David, however, was not frightened, for he knew the Lord was very close to him. 'You came to me with a sword and a spear,' said David, 'but I come to you because you have mocked my God. This is why I shall punish you!'

As he spoke he put a stone in his sling and, before the giant had time to hurl his spear, David swung the stone right at Goliath's forehead.

The stone flew straight through the air and when it struck the giant, he staggered and fell to the ground. It had hit him with such force that it killed him outright. David walked over to where Goliath lay, took the giant's own sword and cut off his head. Never again would Goliath bother the people of Israel or mock the Lord!

The Philistines were shocked but Saul's army was overjoyed. They came running and chased their enemies away. They shouted and cheered and were no longer afraid because God had helped David. The war was over and David was called before the king. 'Stay with me,' said King Saul. 'You are strong and brave. You may now be in charge of some of my soldiers. Do not go back to your sheep for I need you here in the palace.'

King Saul's son, Jonathan, was also there and liked David very much. He gave him presents, including his sword, his beautiful coat, his handsome belt and his bow and arrows. 'Let us always be friends,' said Jonathan.

David wanted to be Jonathan's friend too. It had been a wonderful day. David was now the friend of the king and his son. But he was also the Lord's friend and this was most important.

David runs away from Saul

Read: 1 Samuel 18–20

David was no longer a shepherd. Now he was a general and commander of many soldiers. When enemies came to Canaan he fought them. He fought well because the Lord was on his side. David now lived in a beautiful house close to the king's palace, and often he would eat with the king. The king's daughter became his wife and Prince Jonathan was his best friend. David was an important man and the people who met him on the street bowed to him and said 'David is the bravest and strongest of all!'

Even though David was enjoying many new and wonderful things, he did not become proud but kept on loving the Lord. 'I am not strong,' he thought. 'I cannot do very much alone, but when the Lord helps me I can do what he commands.'

There had been another war and once again David and his soldiers had been victorious . Everyone in Canaan was celebrating and, when David came home the people were waiting to greet him in the street. The women and the young girls walked in front of him in a long parade, and they were so glad the war was over that they made music and sang a special song: 'Saul has beaten a thousand enemies, but David has defeated ten thousand!'

When Saul heard this he became angry and jealous. Every day the words of the song kept going through his mind, and at night he couldn't sleep when he thought of David's popularity. Now he knew who the next king was going to be. He had seen it in the eyes of the people, for they loved David. He could also see it in David himself, for David loved the Lord with all his heart.

'The people want to put me off my throne,' thought Saul. 'They want to make David king.'

Again he had one of his wild fits of temper, stomping his feet as he walked around the palace in a rage. His servants were afraid of him. David, however, was not afraid; rather he felt sorry for King Saul. One day he slipped quietly into the king's room to play some soothing music. He sat in a corner and played his most beautiful songs. This time, however, David was unable to help Saul, who didn't get better, no matter how well David played.

Saul glared at David thinking, 'I will kill him! Then he will never become king!' Suddenly, he picked up his spear and threw it at David. He missed, but it slammed into the wall close to David's head. Terrified, David ran outside, thankful that the Lord had saved his life.

Clearly, David could no longer stay with the king. Even Jonathan agreed that David should go as far away as possible, where Saul couldn't find him. If he did find him surely he would try to kill David again.

Jonathan and David met outside the city in the fields where the two friends said goodbye. Perhaps they would never see each other again and they were very sad. They put their arms around each other and tears ran down their cheeks.

'Be patient, David,' said Jonathan. 'Some day you will become king in spite of my father. It is the Lord's will and I want it too. Will you be good to me and to my children when you become king?'

David hated to leave his friend and promised with all his heart to do as Jonathan had asked. He then fled from the city, away from the king, while Jonathan went back to the palace. David didn't know where to go for the king would try to catch him wherever he went. But he knew that the Lord would take care of him and this gave him peace and rest in his heart.

David shows his love for the King

Read: 1 Samuel 24

David could not return to his own house because Saul wanted to kill him. Neither could he return to his family home for the king was sure to look for him there. He moved from place to place: the desert, the woods or the mountains. Nowhere was safe, for the king was looking everywhere. King Saul hunted for David as a hunter hunts for a wild animal. There were times when he nearly caught him but the Lord watched over David.

On one occasion, David hid deep in a cave in the side of a mountain so that Saul would not find him. Saul looked around the area close to the cave. David and his friends sat quietly. The king was so close they didn't dare speak or even whisper! The soldiers approached the mouth of the cave unaware that David was inside.

When Saul saw the cave he said, 'That cave will be nice and cool. I'll lie down for a while and rest.' He told his men to rest in the shadow of the mountain while he went into the cave. When David and his men saw the king at the entrance, they held their breath. But Saul didn't see them and soon lay fast asleep.

David and his men relaxed a little when they saw that Saul was asleep. They laughed, 'Now our enemy is at our mercy. Punish him, David, for his wickedness! Kill him and you will be king.'

But David didn't want to become king in this way. 'I don't want to be a murderer,' he said. 'God himself will punish King Saul.'

After a while David crept over to the king. Taking his sword he cut off a small piece of Saul's coat and then tiptoed back to his friends. Later, Saul woke up and left the cave to continue to search for David. They hadn't gone very far when David came out of hiding and called out: 'My lord the king!' Saul looked round and was amazed! Where could David have come from so quickly?

'My lord the king, why are you so angry with me?' asked David. 'I haven't done you wrong, have I? I could have killed you a short while ago but I didn't. I only cut off a small piece of your coat.' Then he held out the piece of cloth for Saul to look at.

King Saul was very ashamed of himself. Tears came to his eyes and he cried, 'David, my son, I have done you wrong, yet you have been kind to me. I hated you, but you have loved me in return.' Then Saul left with his soldiers for he no longer wanted to harm David.

The Spear and the Water Jug

Read: 1 Samuel 26

Some time later, consumed with fear and jealousy, King Saul forgot how David had spared his life and began to hunt for him again. One day, when Saul had been searching for a long time without success, it grew dark. He was exhausted and went to lie down in the tent which the soldiers had put up for him.

Before he lay down he drove a spear into the ground, close to where he would lay his head and placed a jug of water nearby. Now the king felt safe. He had a spear near at hand to protect himself and water in case he became thirsty. Calling a couple of soldiers, he said, 'Stay awake and keep guard. Wake me if something is wrong.' Then he lay down and fell fast asleep.

The soldiers who had come with Saul to look for David were also very tired, including the two he had asked to stand guard. Soon the entire camp was sleeping. Not a single man remained awake.

David and his friend Abishai had seen the king and his soldiers earlier in the evening when they had come close to where David was hiding. In the still of the night, the two men approached the king's camp, each with a sword in his hand. They crept past the sleeping guards right up to Saul's tent where he lay fast asleep. They could have done anything they pleased.

'Shall I kill him for you now?' asked Abishai. 'Surely he deserves it. Look how he has tried to kill you so many times.'

'Don't lay a finger on him!' whispered David. 'The Lord has forbidden it. God made him king and he will punish him if he so wishes.' But David took Saul's spear and water jug before the two of them vanished into the night, away from the camp.

In the morning, at sunrise, David climbed a mountain near Saul's camp. He shouted at the top of his voice to the soldiers below, waking them from their sleep. 'Why didn't you take better care of your king? He could have been dead by now. Look! I have his spear and his water jug. I could have harmed him, but I did not!'

King Saul also woke up. 'Is that you, David?' he asked.

'Yes, O King,' replied David. 'Why are you hunting for me all the time? I haven't done you any harm. Last night I stood next to you while you were sleeping but didn't put out my hand to harm you. Now do you believe I'm not your enemy?'

The king hung his head in shame. 'I'm sorry for what I have done. I am an evil man. Come with me to my palace and never again will I try to harm you.' But David was afraid to trust Saul as he knew that the king would soon forget his promise. A soldier came to fetch the king's spear and water jug and took them back to Saul before he returned to his palace. David went to another land where the king couldn't find him, and they never saw each other again.

David becomes King

Read: 2 Samuel 1–2

David lived far away from the palace of Saul. One day a messenger came to bring David sad news from the land of Canaan. The Philistines had come again to attack the people of Israel and had started a war. Saul and Prince Jonathan had taken all their soldiers to fight the Philistines, and both King Saul and Jonathan had been killed in the battle.

When he received the message, David knew that he no longer had to hide. No one would try to hunt for him anymore because his enemy was dead.

Nevertheless, David was very sad to hear the news for he was very fond of the king, despite the fact that he had tried to kill him. Jonathan had been his close friend and the news of his death in particular grieved him very much.

David wept and could neither eat nor drink. When evening came he took his harp and sang a song in mourning for King Saul and Prince Jonathan.

David became king of Israel as foretold many years before, when Samuel visited his home in Bethlehem, while he was still a shepherd boy.

After he was crowned, he went to live at the palace in Jerusalem where he ruled over the whole kingdom.

He was a man after God's own heart and David loved the Lord.

Often he would remember how well the Lord had looked after him, had helped him time and time again, and had protected him from harm.

Sometimes he would pick up his harp to play and sing just as he had done many years before, when he was still a shepherd boy tending his father's sheep.

Prince Absalom

Read: 2 Samuel 15–18

King David had a son whose name was Absalom. He was a very handsome prince who was well-liked. He thought to himself, 'If I were king, I would live in the palace and be ruler of the whole land. I would be the richest and most powerful person in Israel.' But David, his father, was king, and he would have to die before Absalom could take over the throne. 'What a long time to have to wait,' he thought. 'I wish my father would get sick and die.'

The people were unaware of Absalom's thoughts for they could only see what the prince wanted them to see. He always seemed a kind person and the people admired him.

David remained very healthy and showed no signs of dying to allow his son to succeed him. The prince began to get impatient. He made up his mind to find a way to have David killed. With a few of his friends, he plotted against his father. 'Go ahead!' they told him. 'You can count on us to help you.'

Having made his plans he went to his father and asked, 'Father, may I go away for a few days? I want to bring an offering to the Lord in Hebron.'

King David was delighted and sent his son off to Hebron, a city not far from Jerusalem. As soon as the prince arrived in the city, he called all the people together to help him. They formed an army and Absalom led them back to Jerusalem to put his father off the throne. When they reached the palace, his servants blew their horns and shouted, 'Absalom is king in Hebron!'

David could not believe it when he heard of the plot against him. He couldn't understand why his own son would do such a thing and it grieved him greatly. 'Must I prepare my servants and my soldiers to fight against my own son? No, I will flee from him. The Lord sees and knows all things. If He wants me to be king he will bring me back to Jerusalem.'

With his head bowed in dismay David left the palace, crying as he walked through the streets. His friends and servants went with him, and many others who supported him followed. They made their way from the city and walked towards the mountains, where they sought shelter from their enemies.

Absalom rode into Jerusalem with his army and took over the throne. Although he was now king he was still not content as he did not have all that he wanted. Above all, he was afraid that his father might return with an army. So he decided that he would look for David and throw him into prison, for only then would he feel really safe.

Absalom marched with his army to the mountains where David and his friends were in exile.

David had no alternative but to send his army off to do battle with Absalom's men. He couldn't bring himself to go with them so he stayed behind in the hills and waited for news of the battle.

Despite his son's treachery, he still loved him very much: 'I hope nothing happens to Absalom. I hope he won't be killed. Please don't harm my son,' he told his soldiers.

The two armies met in a big forest and there they began to fight. Absalom rode ahead of his soldiers and fought with all his strength.

Although he had a good army, David's men were much stronger, because the Lord was helping them. The battle was soon over and Absalom and the remains of his army ran away as fast as they could.

As Absalom fled through the forest his long hair got caught in the branches of a tree. The donkey he was riding kept on running but Absalom was left hanging . His beautiful long hair had been the cause of his undoing. David's men caught up with him and killed him as he hung helpless.

Meanwhile, David waited impatiently for news of the battle which he knew was going on somewhere in the forest. A man came running towards him and shouted, 'O King, we have won the battle!'

'And what about my son?' asked David, anxiously. But the soldier could give him no news. Then another came in to tell him of Absalom's death.

David wept openly and wrung his hands in grief for his dead son. 'Oh, my son Absalom! My son, my son! How I wish you were alive and I had died in your place!'

King David went back to Jerusalem to live in the palace. Once more he sat on his throne and everything was as it had been before. Every time David thought of Absalom he grew sad again for he loved his son, even though he had plotted against him.

King Solomon

Read: 1 Kings 1 and 3

When David died, his son Solomon became king of Israel. King Solomon wanted very much to be a good king and he worried about the task that lay ahead of him. As he was still a young man when he took over the throne, he was anxious that he would not be able to take care of his people. 'This work is much too hard for me,' thought Solomon. 'I am not nearly old enough, nor wise enough, to do the job properly.'

One day Solomon brought an offering to the Lord and then went to sleep. While he was sleeping God spoke to him. 'Solomon, I am going to give you a gift. You may choose whatever you would like to have. No matter what you ask for I will give it to you.'

'How wonderful,' thought Solomon. But what should he ask for? Should he ask the Lord to make him rich? Or should he ask to become great and powerful? Or to live for a very long time? But Solomon asked the Lord, 'Give me wisdom so that I may be a good king.'

'Very well, Solomon,' God said, 'I will make you wiser and more understanding than any man who has ever lived. Because you have chosen so well I will also make you rich, strong and powerful. If you always obey me, I will also give you a long life.'

When Solomon woke up, he was no longer afraid or restless but glad to be king, now that he knew that God would give him wisdom and strength to be the ruler of his people.

One day King Solomon was in his palace when two women came with a quarrel which they wanted the king to settle.

Each woman carried a baby. One of the babies was happy and lively but the other lay lifeless in the mother's arms.

'The living baby is mine,' one of the women said. 'No, it is mine,' protested the other. King Solomon interrupted the argument and told the two women to tell him the whole story.

The first mother began, 'This woman and I live together in the same house. We each had a baby, but last night one of them died. It is her baby who died and the living child is mine.'

But the other argued, 'No, the living baby is mine, and the dead one is hers!'

They both knew the truth but the lying one did not confess, and it was hard to find out which baby belonged to whom. Solomon had to decide which of the women could keep the living baby, so he asked, 'Do both of you want the living child?'

'Yes, your majesty,' said the first. 'Certainly, sir,' said the other. On hearing this King Solomon said something very unusual to the two women. 'All right,' he said, 'we will cut the living baby in half. In this way you can have an equal share.'

Of course the king didn't mean what he had said but the women thought he was serious. Then he called a servant with a large sword and commanded, 'Cut the baby in half!'

Grabbing the child with one hand, the servant raised his sword. 'Oh no! Please don't!' cried one of the women. 'Don't hurt the baby. Give the baby to her, but please let it live!'

But the other woman didn't care. 'Go ahead,' she said, 'cut the baby in half, then neither of us will have anything!'

When he heard this, the king knew which of the women was the real mother. 'Give the child to the first woman,' he said, 'for she loves it dearly and would rather lose it than have it dead!'

The child was given to the real mother and she went home happily with her baby. All the people said, 'How wise King Solomon is!'

Solomon was king for many years and he ruled his people well. He was known not only for his wealth but also for his wisdom and faithfulness to the Lord. As a mark of his love for God he built a beautiful temple, a place where people from all over the country would come to worship and present their offerings.

Elijah and King Ahab

Read: 1 Kings 17

The people of Israel were unhappy. A wicked king called Ahab and his wife Jezebel had taken over the throne and they did not rule the country well. King Ahab and Queen Jezebel said, 'We don't love the Lord God. We want to worship another god.' Then they made themselves an idol called Baal and knelt down to pray before it as their priests brought offerings. They told the Israelites, 'You must also pray to Baal. Forget about the God of your forefathers!'

Because the king had commanded it, the people felt that they should obey, and that it must be all right. But by bowing to this idol they were disobeying the word of the Lord and because of their disobedience, things began to go terribly wrong.

One day the king was sitting on his throne when suddenly the door opened and a strange-looking man came in. He wore a long grey coat with a leather belt around his waist and, to the king's astonishment, he spoke directly to him with a stern look in his eyes.

'I am Elijah, the servant of God. The Lord has sent me to bring you punishment for your sins. The punishment will be this: there will be no more rain in the country, nor will there be any dew at night until I say so!'

Having passed on the message, Elijah turned and walked out of the palace as quickly as he had come in. Everyone was stunned and for a moment no one said a word. The king and his servants were startled at first by the words spoken by the stranger, but then they began to laugh. 'What a funny man!' they said. 'He thinks he can hold back the clouds and the rain!'

But many days and weeks passed without rain. Each day the sun burned like a huge fire in the sky and everything on the earth dried up. The grass withered, the flowers faded and the leaves fell from the trees to blow away in the scorching breeze. The people needed wheat to make bread, but the crops had dried up in the drought and they had nothing to eat. Soon there was famine everywhere, but still the rain didn't come.

When the king saw that Elijah had spoken the truth he became afraid. 'It's Elijah's fault!' he cried. 'He's the one who's caused this. Look everywhere and bring him to me.'

While the people of Israel were suffering from thirst and hunger, Elijah was hiding beside a small river in the mountains. The Lord had shown him where to go to keep away from King Ahab. Elijah slept in a cave near the stream and the Lord took care of him. He did not go hungry, for each morning and evening God sent ravens to bring him food. They dropped pieces of bread and meat at the entrance to the cave so that he could have food every day.

The people of Israel suffered greatly from hunger and thirst because they had forgotten God; but Elijah had enough to eat and drink because he had remained a faithful servant of the Lord.

Elijah and the widow

Read: 1 Kings 17

For a long time Elijah remained in the cave in the mountains. But a time came when even the stream began to dry up because there was no rain and Elijah had to move on. The Lord told Elijah to travel to another country, where he would meet a woman who would help him. After many days' journey, Elijah reached the country the Lord had told him about. He was thirsty and hungry after the long trek, when he met a woman who was gathering firewood. '

Would you bring me some water to drink? I'm terribly thirsty,' he asked the woman. When she kindly brought him something to drink, Elijah said, 'And would you also give me a little bread to eat as I am very hungry?'

She shook her head when Elijah asked her for bread, 'No sir, I cannot, for I have no more bread in the house. I have a bowl with only a handful of flour and a jar with just a few drops of oil and this is all I have. I have just gathered a few sticks so that I can bake just one more roll for my little boy and myself, then that will be the end of it.'

She believed that she and her son were about to die. To her surprise, Elijah said, 'Go home and bake, then come and bring it to me. Then you will be able to bake more for your son and yourself. There will be plenty, for the Lord has told me that the flour in the bowl will not be used up, nor will the oil in your bottle run out. The three of us will eat rolls made of these things until the rains come again and there is enough food to eat.'

These were amazing words but the woman believed them! Taking her armful of sticks home she made a fire in her open stove and with the remaining flour and oil she baked as her son watched. To the mother's great surprise, there was still flour in the bowl and oil in the jug. She almost wept with joy, she was so happy that the Lord had performed such a great miracle.

The woman kept baking, first for Elijah and then for herself and her son. The Lord had kept his word and was taking care of them.

Some time later, while Elijah was still with the woman and her boy, a very sad thing happened. The boy became ill. His breathing became slower and slower until finally it stopped altogether.

The mother was extremely upset by her boy's death and she cried for a very long time. She sat with him in her arms and called his name over and over, but it was no use. Her son was dead and would soon have to be buried.

Elijah felt sorry for the mother and asked her to give him the child. Taking the dead boy from her lap, he laid him on the bed in his room. Then he knelt beside him. 'If the Lord has allowed the boy to die, then surely he can bring him back to life.' He then began to pray, 'Lord, my God, let this child live!'

The Lord heard the prayers of his servant and the boy began to breathe again. He opened his eyes and lifted his head. Overjoyed, Elijah took the boy back to his mother. She did not know what to say. How could this be? The boy hugged his mother and she wept openly with joy. 'Now I know that you're a great prophet and a true servant of the Lord!' she said to Elijah.

Elijah and the Priests of Baal

Read: 1 Kings 18

Elijah stayed at the widow's house for a long time and still not a drop of rain fell in Israel. This was the punishment given to King Ahab and the disobedient people of Israel. For more than three years almost nothing grew on the land. Finally the punishment ended.

'Go to King Ahab,' the Lord told Elijah. 'I am going to send rain again.' Elijah did as he was told and went to the king. The king was very angry when he saw Elijah.

'So there you are!' he shouted. 'You're the one who's given us all this trouble and caused this drought and famine.'

'No!' replied Elijah. 'It wasn't I who troubled Israel, but you! You are the man who forgot the Lord and prayed to the idol Baal. Now listen, and I will tell you what you must do. Call the people together along with the priests of Baal and bring them to a high mountain.'

King Ahab was very afraid of Elijah and he didn't dare disobey him, so he gathered the people and the priests by the high mountain.

'Now I will show you that the Lord is our God!' Elijah told the people. 'You must never forget him again. The Lord can do all things and Baal can do nothing. Now listen, for this is what we will do. The priests of Baal will prepare an offering and I will do the same. We will not, however, burn our offerings. First, the priests of Baal will pray to their God to send fire for their offering. Then I will pray to the Lord to send fire for my offering. The God who sends the fire from heaven will be our God!'

The people agreed. The priests of Baal began their work by piling stones to make an altar. Then they placed wood on the stones and meat on top of the wood. This was to be their offering. Then they began to pray, calling, 'Baal, O Baal, hear us! Give us fire, O Baal! O Baal, answer us!'

But no fire came to burn their offering. Louder and louder they cried, calling, 'Baal, O Baal, answer us!' Still no fire. They grew tired, but still they kept on calling until they were hoarse with all the praying. But Baal did not answer and no fire came down.

Finally, Elijah called to his people, saying, 'Now come near to me and I will begin.' He made an altar also and placed wood on top of the stones. On the wood he placed the meat and then dug a ditch around the pile of stones before he poured water over the entire offering. He made everything soaking wet and water filled the ditch as well.

Elijah then knelt down near the altar and everyone was quiet. It was time for him to pray, but he didn't shout as the priests of Baal had done for he knew the Lord would hear him. Quietly and reverently he prayed, 'Lord God of Abraham, Isaac and Jacob, let the people see that you alone are their God and that I am your servant. O Lord, answer me that they may never again forget you.'

That was all Elijah needed to say. Fire fell from heaven on to the offering and burned it with huge blazing flames. The people ran away from the heat, and the water in the ditch sizzled in the fury of the fire! Seeing this, the people fell on their knees and called out, 'The Lord is our God! The Lord is our God!' They realised how blind and foolish they had been. Baal could do nothing but the Lord could do great things. How could they ever have forgotten the God of their forefathers?

Later, when the people had all left to return to their homes, Elijah remained alone on the mountain. Once again he prayed to the Lord but this time he didn't ask for fire but for rain.

That same evening big clouds came drifting over the land and the rain poured down. The grass became green again and the flowers bloomed once more. The trees put forth new leaves and the wheat grew. As soon as it had ripened the people gathered the harvest.

Naaman and Elisha

Read: 2 Kings 5

There was a little girl who lived with her father and mother in the beautiful land of Canaan. A war had broken out and foreign soldiers invaded the country. They stole and robbed and even took back slaves with them to their own land. One of the slaves was the little girl who became a servant to a great general in the army.

The general's name was Naaman. He gave the little girl to his wife to be her maid. The poor girl was far from home and her parents, but she soon found out that Naaman and his wife were good people and she grew quite fond of them. Naaman was so rich he could have anything he wanted. But even though he was very wealthy he was sad, for he had a terrible disease. There were large swollen sores on his face, hands and feet. Naaman had leprosy and no one could cure him. He grew worse with each passing week and his friends were afraid that he would soon die.

One day the little girl spoke to Naaman's wife. 'In my country where my father and mother live, the master could be cured of his leprosy. There is a prophet in Canaan whose name is Elisha, and he is a servant of God.'

After she had listened to what the little girl had to say, Naaman's wife told her husband about Elisha. 'Is it really possible for me to get well again?' Naaman wondered. He decided to go to the land of Canaan immediately.

Naaman rode in a beautiful carriage and took expensive presents of gold and silver to give to Elisha. It was a long journey but finally Naaman came to the river Jordan. He and his servants crossed into Canaan and soon arrived at Elisha's house.

'Elisha will be very happy to have such a rich man coming to him,' thought Naaman. 'He will probably run to the door and bow before me. Maybe he will pray with me and gently touch the swellings on my body to cure me of the leprosy.'

But Elisha didn't come out of the house at all. He sent a servant to speak to Naaman: 'Go to the river Jordan and wash yourself seven times. When you have done that you will be healed.' Then the door closed again and Naaman was left standing outside, angry and disappointed.

'Did I come all this way just to wash myself in the river Jordan?' he said. 'This won't make me well! Let's go back to my own country where there are more pleasant rivers to bathe in.'

But Naaman's servants were disappointed. They wanted to see their master healed so they asked him, 'Why are you so angry? You could at least try it, couldn't you? Wash yourself in the river seven times and perhaps you will be cured.'

They managed to persuade Naaman to do what Elisha had asked him to do. It certainly wouldn't hurt to try and perhaps it would work. When he came to the banks of the Jordan, Naaman took off his fine clothes, and entered the water.

The first, second and third times he washed himself it made no difference at all. But he did not give up. Four, five, six times he washed. When he came up out of the water the seventh time he jumped and danced for joy, for the swellings had disappeared! His hands and feet were no longer deformed and he felt well again. It was a miracle. Naaman was amazed that Elisha was such an amazing man with such wonderful powers.

But it wasn't Elisha who had cured the leprosy. He was only the servant of God who had prayed for Naaman to be made well again. Naaman wanted to offer Elisha some of the expensive gifts he had brought for him. 'Pick whatever you'd like,' he said. 'Take whatever you want of the gold, silver or the fine clothes.'

But Elisha shook his head and said, 'I want nothing at all. I didn't make you well and you do not need to thank me. You must thank the Lord, for it was he who healed you.'

'Then I will bring the Lord an offering,' said Naaman. 'I want to love him forever and I will always remember him.'

The beautiful presents were then carefully put back into the carriage and Elisha went back into his house as Naaman left to return to his own country. As the coach drove off into the distance, Gehazi, Elisha's servant stood watching, thinking about all the expensive gifts. He was surprised that his master had turned down the offer of such wealth. If Naaman had asked him, he wouldn't have refused the chance to become a rich man.

As he stood watching the coach disappear Gehazi decided to run after it. He caught up with Naaman and his servants, 'Stop! Wait a minute!'

When Naaman heard the servant calling, he stopped the coach and jumped down. 'What's the matter?' he asked. 'Is something wrong?'

'Sir,' answered Gehazi, 'Elisha would like a gift after all! He would like a bag full of silver and two of those nice coats. He has just received two visitors and he'd like to give them something.'

'That's quite all right,' said Naaman. Then he gave Gehazi two bags of silver and two of the fine coats.

Gehazi was very pleased with himself. Now he was rich and could buy anything he wanted. But first he had to hide the presents so that Elisha would not know what he had done. Then he went home and behaved as if nothing had happened.

'Where have you been, Gehazi?' asked Elisha.

'I didn't go anywhere,' he replied, afraid to tell the truth.

Elisha shook his head and said, 'Gehazi, you thought no one saw you. The Lord saw what you did. Do you really believe that money and fine clothes can make you happy? Because of what you have done, you will become very unhappy, for the leprosy which Naaman once had will now afflict you.'

Gehazi's face, hands and feet began to swell up and the leprosy spread all over his body. Soon he became very ill. Gehazi had the fine gifts and was wealthy, but because he had forgotten God he would not be able to enjoy them.

Naaman put his trust in God and lived to enjoy life to the full. He would never again forget the Lord.

Jonah and the City of Nineveh

Read: Jonah 1–4

Jonah was a servant of God who preached to the people of Israel about how they should please the Lord. One day God said to him, 'Jonah, I want you to go to the city of Nineveh. The people there do many wrong things. You must warn them that I shall punish them unless they mend their ways.' But Jonah thought, 'Let them sin and be punished. They are the enemies of my people. I don't want to go to deliver a message to them and save them.'

So he decided that he would not go to Nineveh with the warning from God. Instead, he went in the opposite direction. God had told him to go east but Jonah went west to get as far away from the place as possible.

'I will run far away where God cannot find me. Then I won't have to go to Nineveh.'

Jonah walked until he reached the sea. There he found a ship which was just getting ready to set sail. 'I'll go on board,' thought Jonah. 'It will take me still further away and God will never be able to find me.'

The captain didn't mind if Jonah sailed with his ship, as long as he paid his fare like any other passenger. It was a beautiful day when they left port. The sky was blue and the sun shone brightly.

However, Jonah was not up on deck with the others. He was tired and had gone below to the bottom of the ship where he fell fast asleep. He was trying to hide from God but the Lord saw Jonah in the hold of the ship and had plans for him.

They were not very far out at sea when black storm clouds gathered, hiding the sun. Soon a wind blew up and the waves got higher and began to buffet against the side of the ship. The storm got steadily worse and the ship was in danger of sinking. The captain and his crew were hardy sailors but they had never experienced a storm like this before. They were terrified. But Jonah slept down below, unaware of the commotion on deck.

The captain went to him and shook him, saying, 'How can you sleep like this? Wake up and help us. Pray to your God to save us from the storm, or else we will all drown!'

Jonah went up on deck, where he saw the huge waves and the big black clouds. He heard the howling of the wind and knew the Lord had found him. 'It is my fault that the storm has come,' he said. 'The Lord has sent it because I have done wrong. I was told to go to the east, but I went to the west. I have been disobedient and I tried to run away from God, but it was foolish. Nobody can hide from God! Take me and throw me into the sea. This will be my punishment and I have deserved it. The sea will be quiet again after I am gone, for the Lord will call back the storm.'

But the crew didn't want to throw Jonah overboard. Instead they sailed on, trying to get to shore. The wind blew harder and harder, and the sea roared higher and stronger until the waves almost engulfed the ship. No matter how hard the sailors tried to bring the ship to shore, they couldn't. Having tried everything else, they finally took Jonah and threw him into the sea.

As soon as Jonah was gone the wind dropped and the sea became calm. When the men saw this they said, 'How powerful God is!

Even the wind and the sea obey him.' They were overawed, and grateful that he hadn't allowed their ship to sink.

Jonah was sure that he was going to drown but God had other plans. God sent a large fish to swallow him. It wasn't pleasant in the stomach of the fish but at least he was alive. Inside the fish he thought about what he had done. He knew that he had not been a faithful servant of the Lord. 'God sees me and can hear me I am sure. Now, I will promise always to obey the Lord.'

God sent the fish to the shore where it spat Jonah on to a beach. Again the Lord told Jonah, 'You must go to the city of Nineveh. When you get there I will tell you what to say.'

This time Jonah immediately began to travel in the right direction. When he reached Nineveh God told him to tell the people that in forty days the city would be destroyed. 'It is just what those wicked people deserve,' Jonah thought as he walked through the streets calling out God's message to the people.

Everyone, from the king in his palace, to the men and women in the streets and market-places, shook with fear. They knew that they had done many wrong things and deserved to be punished.

The king told his subjects, 'We must pray and ask God to forgive us. We must repent of our sins and do no more evil.' So that was exactly what they did. All the men, women and children prayed to God for mercy. He heard them and saw that they were really sorry so he did not punish Nineveh.

During this time, Jonah sat on a hillside not far from the city. The people of Nineveh were his enemies and he wanted to see their city in ruins. He had no pity at all. Jonah waited and waited but, to his surprise, nothing happened. He was disappointed and angry that he had come all this way to see his enemies punished, only to have God forgive them and save the city. God wanted to take the hatred from Jonah's heart and so he gave him a sign.

A tree began to grow next to Jonah. It grew quickly until it became big enough for him to shelter from the scorching sun. Jonah was pleased that God had sent the tree to protect him.

But the next morning, the tree died. God had sent a worm to eat through the roots so that it could not get water to grow. Jonah could not find a place to shade from the sun and he became angry with God for allowing this to happen to the tree.

'Jonah,' God said, 'You feel sorry for a tree! May I not have pity on all those men, women and children in Nineveh?'

Jonah was ashamed of himself and realised how wise, kind and merciful God was to save the people of Nineveh.

The good King Hezekiah

Read: 2 Kings 18–20

Once there lived a young prince called Hezekiah who loved God. After his father died, Hezekiah became king of Israel. The people of Israel, however, had forgotten the Lord and worshipped idols. They no longer thought about God, nor visited the temple in Jerusalem which Solomon had built as a house for the Lord. They had even nailed up the temple doors so that no one could get in.

Every year their enemies came to attack them. This was the punishment they had to suffer for having forgotten the Lord. But when Hezekiah became king, he knew that his people were doing wrong. 'We can't go on like this,' he said to the people. 'We must serve the Lord again and truly be the people of God. I will do all in my power to make this happen.'

Hezekiah immediately went to work and had all the idols smashed to pieces. He sent men to re-open the doors to the great temple in Jerusalem and had the house of the Lord cleaned from top to bottom. Then he sent his servants through the land, calling all the people to Jerusalem. 'Now we will all bring offerings,' he said. 'We will go to the house of God and ask the Lord to forgive us our sins.'

Hezekiah was a strict king but a good one, and the people did as they were told. When they brought their offerings to the Lord they also celebrated with a huge feast. The days which followed were wonderful for the people of Israel. They now wanted to love God and in doing so they became strong and happy. They were truly God's people again.

Hezekiah went out with his army and attacked his enemies, so that they wouldn't come back to bother the Israelites. But Hezekiah wasn't satisfied. There was so much that he wanted to do to ensure that the nation became stronger, and that the people would love the Lord even more.

Suddenly, in the middle of all his work, Hezekiah became very ill. He grew worse and worse and none of his doctors could find a cure. Hezekiah became very sad for he wanted to be well enough to continue the work he had started. When he was thinking about these things the door to his room opened. Isaiah, the prophet, a servant of the Lord, came in to deliver a message from God to the king. But it was a very sad one.

'My king, the Lord has said that the time has come for you to say goodbye to your family and friends for soon you will die.'

Hezekiah wasn't afraid to die for he dearly loved God and knew he would go to be with him. Nevertheless it saddened him very much because he still had many things to do for his people. His great work for God wasn't finished yet.

After Isaiah left, Hezekiah turned his face to the wall and sobbed out his terrible grief. 'O Lord,' he cried, 'let me live just a little longer! Allow me to continue working for my people. I do so want to make them happier and stronger.'

A little while later the door opened and in came Isaiah again. This time he brought a happy message for the king. 'The Lord says, "I have heard your prayer and I have seen your tears. I will make you well, and you will live for another fifteen years. I will also help you overcome your enemies."'

This news was so wonderful Hezekiah could hardly believe his ears. As God had promised, three days later the king was well again. The first place he visited was the house of God. The Lord had done a wonderful thing for King Hezekiah and he wanted to say thank-you.

A few years later the Lord showed Hezekiah an even greater wonder. A foreign king had come with a large army to attack Jerusalem. They wanted to destroy the city, to rob and set fire to all the houses, and then capture King Hezekiah.

Around Jerusalem was a high wall which the enemy soldiers would have to climb before they could capture the city. The Israelites closed and bolted the doors as soon as they saw the enemy coming. The army camped around the walls and laid siege to the city so that no one could get in or out. There they waited for a long time, making sure that no food could be brought into the city.

It was a very desperate time for the people of Jerusalem. They still had a little food but, if the soldiers didn't leave soon, there would be nothing left to eat and they would have to open the gates. Everyone, including the king, feared for their lives.

'There is someone who can help us,' said Hezekiah and he went to the temple where he prayed to the Lord. 'O Lord, please help us and save Jerusalem from destruction!'

A short time after he had prayed, Isaiah came to the king and said, 'Don't be afraid for the Lord has said that he will help you. Your enemies will not get into Jerusalem.'

A little later, a letter came from the enemy king making fun of the Lord. In it he wrote, 'Do not believe that your God will help you. He is unable to save you! Don't let God fool you any longer, for I am much stronger than He is!'

Hezekiah decided to take the letter to the temple, where he opened it before the Lord for he knew that only God could answer it. God did just that and, when night fell, an angel came down from heaven and passed through the enemy camp like a plague. The angel brought God's answer to the letter by bringing a terrible punishment.

In the morning more than a hundred thousand soldiers lay dead. The ones who were left were so terrified that they ran straight back to their own country. Never again would they dare to come back to Jerusalem, for they were very afraid of the God of Hezekiah. No other enemies attacked Israel while Hezekiah was alive and the people of Israel lived happily and in peace.

The Israelites in Babylon

Read: Daniel 1–2

After King Hezekiah died everything went wrong again in Israel. Other kings came to the throne who didn't love the Lord. They worshipped idols. The people of Israel did as their rulers said, forgetting about the God of their forefathers. The Lord had been patient with his people for a long time, and he had often warned them through the prophets that they would be punished if they did not heed his words.

Foreign armies invaded Israel and destroyed Jerusalem. They burned Solomon's beautiful temple and took the people away as prisoners to Babylon, the enemy's homeland. The Israelites became slaves of the Babylonians for a long time until the Lord was no longer angry with them.

The king of Babylon was called Nebuchadnezzar. He lived in a magnificent palace with many servants. Among the servants were four important young men taken from Israel; one was called Daniel.

It was difficult and dangerous to be a servant of Nebuchadnezzar. He was a proud and severe ruler. If a servant displeased him, he would have his head cut off. Nebuchadnezzar was very powerful and his word was law. However, Daniel and his friends were not afraid. They loved the Lord and knew that he would protect them.

One night Nebuchadnezzar had a strange dream. He woke up with a start, his heart thumping with fear and he couldn't get back to sleep again. What was worse, he was unable to remember what the dream had been about. But he believed there must be some hidden meaning. King Nebuchadnezzar had many wise and learned men whom he consulted when he needed guidance. The next morning he sent for them and told them about his strange experience in the middle of the night. 'I have had a dream and I must know what it means.'

The wise men bowed deeply before the king and answered, 'Your majesty, tell us your dream and we will explain it.'

'No,' said the king, 'You are the wise men. You tell me what the dream was and I will reward you with gold. However, if you are not able to tell me what I dreamt, I will put you to death.'

The wise men were terribly afraid and protested, 'Your majesty, no one in the world can tell you what your dream means if you cannot remember it yourself.'

The king was furious. 'You are liars, all of you!' he shouted. 'You say you know everything but you know nothing at all!'

Then he called his soldiers and ordered them to execute all the wise men in Babylon who were unable to tell him about his dream. When they came to the house of Daniel he asked to be taken immediately to King Nebuchadnezzar. 'Wait until tomorrow, your majesty, and I shall be able to tell you what you dreamt during the night,' he said confidently.

The king agreed to wait and Daniel went to speak to his friends. 'Only one knows what the king has dreamt,' he said, 'God himself. We must ask him to tell us.'

They prayed to the Lord together and during the night Daniel had the same dream the king had, but this time God gave him the meaning.

Daniel was very pleased and he thanked God for helping him. Then he quickly returned to the palace to speak to King Nebuchadnezzar.

'Can you really tell me what I dreamt?' asked the king.

'No!' replied Daniel. 'I am not able to do this, for no man can do such a thing, but there is a God in heaven who knows all things. He told me about your dream.'

Then Daniel went on to tell the king about his dream. 'You saw a very great statue,' he said, 'so large that you were amazed by it. The head of the statue was gold and the breast silver. The stomach was made of copper and the legs of iron. The feet were made of iron and clay. Near the statue was a mountain and a stone came rolling down the side of it. The stone hit the feet of the statue and the statue fell. The stone smashed the statue into pieces so small that there was nothing left of it. The stone itself, however, grew bigger and bigger until it was as big as the whole world.

'This was your dream, your majesty, and there is a hidden meaning to it: The stone was stronger than the entire statue in the same way that God is stronger than all the kingdoms of the world. That is what it means!'

King Nebuchadnezzar's eyes were wide with amazement, for now he could remember it all. This was exactly what he had dreamt and he said, 'Daniel, what a mighty God you have!'

He gave Daniel all kinds of expensive and beautiful gifts and gave him an important job to do in the country. Daniel's three friends were also honoured by the king.

Trial by fire

Read: Daniel 3

Daniel's three brave friends served the king well. They knew how severe he could be with people, but they were confident that the Lord would always protect them. Some time after the incident with the dream, King Nebuchadnezzar had a large statue built, a golden image which everyone would have to bow to, not unlike the one that he had seen in his dream. Nearby he had a large furnace constructed which was fired to a great heat. He called his vast army of servants, about a thousand of them, and told them what was soon to happen. 'Attention, all of you. In a short time you will hear music. When it starts to play you must all fall down in front of this great idol and pray to it. If you refuse you will be thrown into the furnace I have made.'

It was very quiet; all you could hear was the roar of the huge fire. Great black clouds of smoke rose to the sky. Everyone was very afraid and, as soon as the music started to play, they all fell on their knees to pray to the image. All, that is, except Daniel's friends, Shadrach, Meshach and Abednego. They refused to bow before the idol. They were sent to the king immediately.

'Did you do that on purpose?' he asked. 'I will give you one more chance. If you don't kneel this time, I shall have you thrown into the furnace. Who will help you then?'

But the men were not afraid and said, 'Your majesty, we cannot kneel before an image, for our God has forbidden us to do such a thing. If you have us thrown into the fire God will be able to help us.'

The king flew into a rage at their disobedience and ordered the fire to be made seven times hotter than normal. Then he called his strongest soldiers and told them to throw the three men into the fire. The heat was so great that even the soldiers who approached the furnace with the men collapsed and died. The king watched the scene intensely as the three men were thrown into the fire. Suddenly his eyes widened. Shielding himself from the heat he gazed into the depth of the furnace and exclaimed loudly, 'Didn't we throw three men into the fire?'

'Yes three,' replied his servants.
'But now there are four,' continued the king. 'Look for yourselves and notice, the fourth one doesn't look like a man, he looks like a god!'

Moving as close as he dared to the furnace, he shouted to the men who seemed to be walking around unharmed despite the heat: 'If you are alive, come out!' The three friends walked out of the furnace as if nothing had happened. Not a single hair on their heads had been burned and their clothes didn't even smell of fire. The three friends had trusted in God and he had protected them from danger. Nebuchadnezzar learned that there was one much more powerful than he was, the God of the Israelites.

Daniel in the Lions' Den

Read: Daniel 6

Daniel lived for many more years and was still in Babylon, where he remained an important servant of the king. King Nebuchadnezzar had died many years before and now there was another king whose name was Darius. King Darius respected Daniel greatly as one of his most faithful servants. He gave him important work to do and made him governor of the kingdom. When some of the other servants heard of this they were jealous of Daniel and plotted against him.

'We don't want this foreigner to rule over us. Let us watch Daniel very carefully to see if he does anything wrong. Then we can tell the king about it and have him removed.'

They secretly spied on Daniel every day, to see if he did anything against the laws of the king. But they could find no fault with him, because he worked hard as an obedient servant. Busy as he was, however, he always found time to pray to God three times a day, kneeling unashamedly in his room in front of an open window.

Far away lay Jerusalem, where the beautiful temple had once stood. Some day the people of Israel would return to their land and another temple would be built. This was Daniel's hope and prayer as he looked out of his window in the direction of Jerusalem. 'Lord, let your people be free again and allow them to go back to their own country to worship you in your holy temple.'

The other servants noticed the fact that Daniel prayed every day. This gave them an idea which they knew would upset him, and would lead to his downfall as the king's favourite servant.

They went to the king and bowed before him. 'Your majesty, we have thought of how to ensure that everyone respects only you as king of this land. You must order all the people to ask nothing from any god or man, for a whole month. They must only ask help from you as the mighty king of Babylon.'
King Darius liked the idea and made it law. 'Any who disobey shall be punished severely and thrown into the den of lions.'

The law was decreed thoughout all Babylon. No one was to pray to any god but had to bow only to King Darius. Daniel, soon heard about the order and he knew very well who had influenced the king. It would be very hard for those who worshipped the God of Israel. But Daniel loved the Lord and, although he was the king's most respected servant, he continued to pray to God three times a day.

In order to trap Daniel, his enemies had spies positioned under his window. As soon as they saw him pray as usual, they

quickly went to the king. 'Your majesty, didn't you say that no one should pray to any god for an entire month?'

'Yes,' answered the king, 'indeed I did.'

'And anyone who disobeyed must be thrown into the lions' den?' the men added.

'Yes,' said the king, 'that is what I ordered.'

'Well, sir,' they continued, 'your servant Daniel must be thrown to the lions, for he has disobeyed you. He prays to his God three times a day. We have proof that he does this.' The king was shocked and dismayed. 'Not Daniel,' he cried. 'No, not Daniel!'

But the men said, 'You said so yourself, O king, and now you must do it, for your word is law!'

A decree of the king could not be broken in Babylon. Whatever the king said, had to be done. No matter how much the king wanted to help Daniel, he could not change the law even for his most respected servant.

When evening came, Daniel was brought to the lions' den. The king was upset that he had been tricked. 'Daniel, I cannot do anything for you but I hope the Lord will help you.' Then Daniel was thrown to the lions.

That night King Darius could not sleep as he thought of Daniel. In his heart he hoped that Daniel's God would save him. First thing in the morning Darius made straight for the lions' den to find out if Daniel was still alive. He shouted in a loud voice, 'Daniel! Daniel!'

To his amazement, a voice came back, 'I am well, your majesty, for the Lord has saved me. The lions did me no harm because I have done no wrong.'

The king was overjoyed to find Daniel alive and unharmed. 'Take him out of there immediately,' he ordered the guards.

When the king remembered how he had been tricked into making this law, he had the servants who plotted against Daniel arrested and thrown into the den of lions in his place.

Then Daniel was put in an even more honoured position than before. In addition, he made it law that everyone in Babylon should serve and worship the God to whom Daniel prayed, and who had saved him from the lions.

The Israelites return

Read: Ezra 1, 3, 5–7

The Israelites were in exile in Babylon for many years. They were ruled by the kings of the country and, although they longed to return home, they were not allowed to. These years of captivity were the result of their disobedience. They had forgotten the Lord who had taken their people out of Egypt long ago, and had led them to the Promised Land. They had also worshipped false gods. Instead of becoming a prosperous, happy nation in Canaan, they were a scattered and sad people.

Finally their punishment came to an end and God allowed them to return home. They set out, a great parade of happy people and, after a very long journey came at last to Canaan. But they were dismayed when they arrived, for all their houses had been burned and the wall around Jerusalem had been broken to pieces. The beautiful temple of Solomon had been burnt to the ground, and nothing was left except a pile of stones.

The people immediately started to work, building houses and rebuilding the temple. They began to repair the city walls and after many years of hard work the task was completed. Finally everyone returned from exile to their country and their new homes. The people of Israel no longer prayed to idols, for they didn't want to forget God again. They prayed only to the Lord and brought offerings to him in the new temple. They also began to read the books written by the prophets about the history of their people and the laws which they must obey.

The New Testament

Zechariah receives the Good News

Read: Luke 1

A man and his wife called Zechariah and Elizabeth lived in a house in the hills of Israel. Zechariah was a priest, whose duty was to tell the people of Israel about the Lord, pray for them and bring offerings to God on their behalf. Zechariah and Elizabeth were good people who loved the Lord dearly. They had no children. Years before, while they were still young, they had often prayed for a child but now they were old and no longer believed that it would be possible for them to have a child.

One day Zechariah had to make a trip to the temple in Jerusalem. He put on his best clothes, his beautiful white priest's robes and set off on his journey. It was a long way to Jerusalem from where he lived, but he finally reached the city and made his way to the temple of the Lord. Many other people were making their way there to worship and pray and to bring offerings to God.

In front of the temple was a large open square where the people bought their offerings. They could buy sheep or doves and then give them to the priests, who would kill them and lay them on the fire, which had been built specially for the purpose. The meat would burn and the smoke would rise to heaven as a sign to God which meant, 'Lord, we love you and we want to give you a gift.'

Another offering was made in the temple, but not everyone could go inside. In fact only one priest could go in and, since all the priests wanted to give the offerings, they drew lots to see who would be the chosen one. On that particular day, Zechariah was the priest chosen to make the offering.

While everyone else waited outside, Zechariah went into the temple very reverently. He entered a large room with walls of gold, where seven golden lamps burned. The light from the lamps shone on the walls and it was very quiet. Zechariah was all alone in the temple of God.

Standing in the golden room with the seven lamps was a golden bowl with little coals of fire in it. Zechariah had to present the offering, so he sprinkled little grains of incense on top of the burning coals. This gave off a sweet smell and was called the incense offering. While Zechariah was busy with the ceremony, he prayed silently for the people waiting outside.

Suddenly he stopped praying! He was startled, because he felt that he was no longer alone. Beside him stood a man in white robes just like those Zechariah was wearing. He wasn't a priest, but an angel who had come to give him a message from the Lord! Zechariah was very afraid and he trembled, but the angel said, 'Don't be afraid, Zechariah, for I have come to bring you good news. Your prayers have been heard and your wife Elizabeth will have a son. You must name him John.'

Zechariah didn't understand how this could be, for he and his wife were old now. He stood there shaking his head in disbelief.

'The child will make you

very happy,' said the angel, 'and many others will be glad also, for he will be a servant of God. When he is grown, he will tell the people that the Saviour is coming.'

This news should have made Zechariah happy, for the people of Israel had waited a long time for the coming of the Saviour, but the old man couldn't believe it! 'No,' he said. 'This can't be so. I'm old and Elizabeth is old, how can I believe such a thing? What you say would be a miracle!'

'I am Gabriel. God himself has sent me to give you this news. I will show you that the Lord can work miracles, and I will also punish you for not believing me. You will be unable to speak a word until all the things I have told you have happened.'

With that, the angel disappeared and Zechariah found himself alone once more in the temple. Outside in the outer court the people stood waiting for the priest to return with the words of blessing. When he did appear, however, he said nothing. He opened his mouth to utter the words of blessing from the Lord but no words came out.

'What has happened to him?' wondered the people. 'What has he seen in the temple that he cannot speak?'

But Zechariah could not explain what had happened. When he had finished all he had to do in the temple, he made his way back home, anxious to give his wife the good news that God had answered their prayers. There was no more doubt in his mind about what the angel had told him and he wanted to sing for joy - but couldn't!

As soon as he arrived home, he took a little piece of slate on which to write and told Elizabeth everything that had happened in the temple. 'His name will be John,' he added at the end.

Less than a year later Zechariah and Elizabeth had a baby boy. When all the neighbours and friends heard about it they were very pleased for the couple, who, they knew longed so much to have a child. When the baby was eight days old they came to visit the priest's home to join in the celebration, for on this day the child would be given his name.

They thought, of course, that the baby would be called Zechariah after his father as was the custom, but Elizabeth told them his name would be John. 'John?' they asked, surprised. 'What a strange name! We will ask Zechariah if this is to be his name.'

'What will the baby's name be?' they asked Zechariah.

Zechariah still couldn't talk, even though he wanted to, so he took his writing slate and wrote, 'His name is John.'

Suddenly Zechariah was able to speak again; everything that the angel had said had come true. 'Yes,' shouted Zechariah. 'John is his name, for the Lord has heard our prayer!' Then he sang for joy, singing a lovely song in honour of God.

'How amazing everything is about this child,' thought the people. 'This is no ordinary baby!' Everywhere they went they told others about Zechariah and Elizabeth and the little boy whose name was John.

The angel comes to Mary

Read: Luke 1

A girl called Mary lived in the village of Nazareth, not far from Jerusalem. Although she lived in an ordinary house she was, in fact, a descendant of King David, the great king who ruled Israel many years before. Nearby lived a young man called Joseph, a carpenter, and he too was a descendant of King David. Mary and Joseph were very much in love and wanted to get married. Although they were both of royal descent they were poor, and would live in an ordinary house after their wedding, not in a palace.

These were hard and cruel times for the people of Israel. But everyone hoped for happier days because the Lord had promised that a child would be born who would grow up to be King and set the people free.

One day Mary was in her house alone when she hear a voice speaking to her. 'Mary, you are the most favoured woman in all the world!' When Mary looked up she saw an angel. It was the angel Gabriel and he wore a bright white robe.

'Don't be afraid, Mary,' he said. 'I am going to tell you something wonderful. The Lord has sent me to you. In a little while you will have a baby son and you will name him Jesus. When the baby is grown he will be King.'

When Mary heard this her heart sang, for then she understood. The child would be the Saviour who would come to save his people and she was to be his mother.

'Who will be the father of the child?' asked Mary. 'I am not yet married.'

'God will be the father,' answered the angel. 'This is why he will not be an ordinary child. He will be a holy child and he will be called the Son of God!'

Mary bowed her head and said, 'Then everything is well. May it all happen just as you have said.'

The angel Gabriel had done his work so he returned to heaven. He had brought the most wonderful message ever to be given to the world.

The baby in the manger

Read: Luke 2

Mary and Joseph married as planned. God had also told Joseph the news about Mary and the special baby that would be born. One day they had to travel to Bethlehem, the city where King David had lived long ago. Everyone was told to go back to where they had been born because the Roman emperor wanted to count all the people in the empire at the time.

It was a long journey to Bethlehem and by the time they arrived Mary was exhausted as she was was expecting her baby soon.

'It's only a little further, Mary,' said Joseph. 'We're almost there, and soon we can find ourselves a place to sleep tonight.'

Together they walked into Bethlehem, but it was almost dark when they came to a big house, an inn, where travellers could rest for the night. However, many people were travelling at that time. The inn was full. Joseph didn't want Mary sleeping outdoors with the baby due. Nearby was a stable which would at least give them shelter and there was straw for them to make a bed to lie on.

That night, the promised baby was born in a stable in Bethlehem. Mary and Joseph were very happy. Mary took some pieces of cloth and wrapped him up to keep him warm. They had no crib either, but Joseph took a manger used for feeding the animals and made a little bed of straw in it for Mary to lay the baby. 'He will be called Jesus,' said Mary. 'This is what the angel said.'

The shepherds of Bethlehem

Read: Luke 2

In the middle of the night in which the Saviour was born, there were some shepherds working in the fields of Bethlehem. The people in the town were sleeping but the shepherds remained awake to guard their sheep.

As the night was cool the shepherds had built a fire and were sitting around it with the sheep sleeping close to them. The stars twinkled over their heads and the wind rustled gently in the grass. All was calm and still.

Suddenly the shepherds were startled, for it seemed as though the sun had begun to shine. In the middle of a very bright light stood an angel who had come from heaven. The shepherds were terrified and hid their eyes.

'Don't be afraid,' said the angel, 'for I have come to tell you something which will make you glad. Tonight the Saviour who is Christ the Lord has been born in Bethlehem. You will find the baby wrapped in soft clothes and lying in a manger.'

Then the sky was filled with a huge choir of angels singing: 'Glory to God in the highest, and peace on earth to all men.'

As the angels sang they soared higher and higher back to heaven. Then all was quiet once again in the fields of Bethlehem. The shepherds, however, didn't go back and sit by their campfire. 'Let's go to Bethlehem, where we can see what the angel has told us about. The Saviour has been born!'

When they came to Bethlehem they found the stable and when they went in, they saw two ordinary people sheltering there. They weren't rich, or noble, or important - in fact they were just like the shepherds really. They told Mary and Joseph what had happened to them in the field while they were looking after the sheep.

Then they saw the baby, an ordinary baby, just like any other they had seen before, but they knew that this was the Saviour. He lay in the manger, wrapped in soft pieces of cloth, just as the angel had said. This was the Saviour who had come to his people. The shepherds then knelt down in front of the manger to worship him.

The baby in the Temple

Read: Luke 2

Joseph and Mary took the baby with them to the temple in Jerusalem. They wanted to tell the Lord how happy they were with the baby and to ask Him to bless and care for the little child. Had they been rich, they would have bought a lamb but they were poor, so they would have to buy two doves instead.

When they arrived in Jerusalem, Mary carried the baby Jesus through the streets. Many people were walking about, but no one paid any attention to the little baby in Mary's arms. No one knew that this little child was really the Saviour for whom they had waited so long.

At the temple, Joseph bought the two doves and gave them to the priest, who held his hands above the child and said, 'The Lord bless you...'

Suddenly an old man came walking straight towards Mary. Tears rolled down his cheeks because he was so happy to see the child in her arms. His name was Simeon, and he knew who the little child was, because God had told him.

Simeon had longed for the coming of the Saviour and had often been sad because it had seemed such a long time to wait. But God had told him, 'Don't be sad, for before you die, you will see the Saviour.'

Now the child was here, the one for whom Simeon had waited so long. He was so happy, he took Jesus in his arms and said, 'Now I am ready to die, Lord, for I am at peace. My own eyes have seen the Saviour!' Then he sang for joy just as the shepherds had done after they had seen the baby Jesus!

Then a little old woman came shuffling along. Her name was Anna and she knew about the Saviour too. As she looked down on Jesus, she cried, 'This is the Saviour! How happy I am for he has come at last!' Anna then hurried down the street to tell everyone that she had seen the Saviour.

After visiting the temple, Mary and Joseph returned home with Jesus, full of joy for all that had happened that day.

The Wise Men from the East

Read: Matthew 2

One night wise men from the East were gazing heavenwards studying the stars, when they noticed that a new one had appeared. It was a big star and it shone brighter than all the others. They stood gazing at it in wonder. 'A new star,' they said. 'That must mean that a child has been born somewhere and it is such a beautiful star it must mean the child is very wealthy and important. It must be the child of a king!'

For a long time they watched the star and then one of them said, 'We must try to find this king so that we can kneel before him for surely there has never been so rich and mighty a king on this earth before.'

So the wise men set off to look for the newborn child. Their servants went to fetch the camels and the wise men prepared beautiful expensive gifts. They even took a chest of gold. Then they mounted their camels and began to journey in the direction of the star.

It was a long journey over high mountains and through great forests. They had to ride through countries that they had never visited before, until they reached Israel. The young king for whom they were looking must be in this land, but how could they find him? They travelled to Jerusalem, the largest city, and on to the palace, where surely a king would have been born.

They requested an audience with King Herod, the cruel leader put there by the Romans. When he heard their story he became alarmed.

How was it that the wise men were looking for the king of the Jews? 'I am the king!' thought Herod. 'And I want to remain king. Can there possibly be another king, a young king who has just been born? This cannot be, for I want to reign alone! I must know where I can find him and then I had better kill him for this child must never become king.'

Herod called on the scribes, who knew all about the sacred writings, to find out from the prophecies where this king would be born. 'It is written that he will be born in Bethlehem,' they told him.

Then the king spoke to the wise men. He asked, 'When did you see this beautiful star?'

'It was a long time ago,' they replied. 'We first saw it when we were still in our own country and we have been looking for the young king ever since but without success so far.'

'Then I will help you,' said king Herod. 'He is in Bethlehem. Go there quickly and look. When you have found him, come and tell me, for I also want to go and kneel before him.'

The wise men didn't know that the king was wicked, and they quickly went on their way to Bethlehem, following the star as they had done before. It led them to Bethlehem where it seemed to stop above a little house.

They got off their camels, opened the door and went inside, where they found Mary and Joseph and the child Jesus. He looked like any other child and they wondered if this was indeed the one they had been looking for.

When they spoke to Mary and Joseph they knew that they had come to the right place. He was no ordinary child but was the one who would be the Saviour of the world.

The wise men knelt before the young king to worship him and gave the presents of gold, sweet-smelling incense and myrrh. These were expensive gifts to bring but they gave them gladly, for they were pleased to have found the one they had been looking for.

When they slept that night in Bethlehem, God spoke to them in a dream. He told them not to return to Jerusalem to King Herod, who wanted to kill the child, but to return home another way. So the wise men set off back to their own country. Their journey had been long and interesting and one that they would never forget.

King Herod

Read: Matthew 2

In the meantime, Herod was wondering why the wise men had not returned to Jerusalem to tell him where the child was in Bethlehem. He was eager to find the baby in order to make sure he would never become king. But God had plans to protect Jesus.

Joseph had a dream in which an angel spoke to him: 'Take the child and his mother and go away from here quickly. Go to Egypt and stay there until I tell you it is safe for you to return.' Joseph woke up and told Mary what the angel had said. They immediately set off on the long journey to Egypt, where they would be safe from Herod.

King Herod was unaware that the baby had escaped as he waited for the wise men to return. Finally his patience ran out when he realised that they were not coming back.

That night he ordered that all baby boys in Bethlehem should be put to death. 'Now there is no chance that the king will still live to take my place,' thought Herod.

After Herod died, an angel told Mary and Joseph that it was safe for them to return to Israel. They made their way back, not to Bethlehem, but to Nazareth where Joseph worked as a carpenter.

Jesus as a boy

Read: Luke 2

When Jesus was a boy he lived in Nazareth with Mary and Joseph. He looked like any other boy but Mary knew in her heart that he was different, for he was the Son of God. Every year Mary and Joseph travelled to Jerusalem to celebrate the Feast of the Passover.

When Jesus was very small he probably stayed at home but, like all Jewish boys, at the age of twelve, he was allowed to go to the feast for the first time. The family travelled together that year to the temple where the feast was held, to bring their offering and pray to the Lord.

The feast lasted for seven days and then everyone would return home. When Mary and Joseph got ready to make the journey back they could not find Jesus anywhere.

They didn't worry at first as he was always sensible and obedient. They thought perhaps he had gone ahead with the other children and they would catch up with him on the road.

They kept a lookout for him as they made their way but were concerned when they did not see him. When evening came and there was still no sign of Jesus, they decided to turn back to Jerusalem to look for him.

They searched for three days and finally looked for him in the temple, which was quiet now that the crowds had gone home.

As Mary looked around she was relieved to see Jesus sitting among the wise old men, listening to what they had to say and asking questions. Never before had they come across a boy who understood them so well and could give such good answers.

Mary ran towards him. 'Jesus,' she said, 'why did you do this to us? Your father and I have been so worried! We have been looking everywhere for you!'

'Why did you look for me?' asked Jesus. 'Didn't you know I must be about my father's business?' Then Mary knew that Jesus hadn't been disobedient. She had worried about him because she had forgotten for a moment all that she knew. They then returned home as a family to Nazareth, where Jesus lived until he grew up.

John the Baptist

Read: Matthew 3

John, the son born to Zechariah and Elizabeth in their old age, grew up to become a servant of God. When he left home to start his ministry he lived in the desert, where God spoke to him and told him what he should do.

People came from all over to hear him preach. 'Repent, turn from your sin and be baptised,' he would say, 'for the Saviour is coming very soon.'

To teach the people that God wanted to give them a clean heart he would take them to the river Jordan to be baptised.

When people heard John preaching, they asked, 'Is this the Saviour, the Messiah for whom we are waiting?'

But John told them that he was not the Messiah but only his servant. 'No, I am not the Saviour. He is greater than I am and I am not worthy even to untie the straps of his sandals!'

When John was preaching one day, Jesus came by, and John was pleased to see him. John was surprised, however, when Jesus asked him to baptise him. Why should someone who was without sin wish to be baptised like other people?

When he questioned Jesus, he insisted that John should do it, so they walked into the water together.

When Jesus came out of the water, a voice came from heaven which said,

'This is my Son, whom I love.'

Then what looked like a white dove came down from the sky and rested on Jesus' head.

The dove was a symbol of the Holy Spirit and John knew without doubt that this was indeed the Lord Jesus, the Saviour of the world.

After Jesus had left to start his ministry, John called to the people, 'Repent, for the kingdom of heaven has come!'

Soon John's work would be over, and the Lord Jesus would tell others about the kingdom of God.

The first disciples

Read: Mark 1 and Luke 5

Jesus was walking along beside the sea when he saw a fishing-boat close to the shore. There were two brothers in it, one called Peter and the other Andrew. He stopped to watch the two men working and shouted to them, 'Come and follow me and I will make you fishers of men.' Andrew and Peter did as they were told, leaving their fishing-boat and their nets to follow Jesus and become his disciples.

A little further along there was another boat which had been pulled up on to the shore while the men mended their nets.

There was an older man and his two sons, James and John. Jesus called the two sons to also leave their nets and follow him.

Later others joined the group until Jesus had twelve disciples. They followed Jesus everywhere and were pleased to become his friends.

Water into Wine

Read: John 2

Jesus was once invited to a wedding along with his mother Mary and some of his disciples. It was a happy occasion, with music, delicious food and good wine to drink. However, in the middle of the feast, the wine ran out, but only a few people were aware of it. Mary got to know about it and told Jesus, who spoke to the servants.

He asked them to fill six large jugs with water then pour some out for the guests. The servants did as they were told and when they poured it they were surprised to see that wine flowed out. 'Surely this is no ordinary man,' they said to each other as they took the wine to the guests.

The guests knew nothing about what had happened but commented to their host, 'Most people offer the best wine first, but you have saved it for the last!'

Jesus reaches out to others

Read: Luke 5 and John 21

The Lord Jesus travelled widely with his disciples, preaching and healing the sick. Many who were blind came to him; along with others who could not walk or who had diseases which could not be cured. He welcomed everyone who came to him.

There were also those who came to share their worries with him and to ask him how they could have eternal life. Then he would pray with them and tell them that he had come to earth to forgive their sins and bless them. But first they had to turn from their sins and trust in him.

They came from far and near in their hundreds, and sometimes in their thousands, to hear what he had to say.

Although the crowds often flocked to meet him, Jesus always had a special place in his life for the disciples and liked to spend time with them alone.

Once, when they came near to the seashore where Jesus first called the fishermen to follow him and become his disciples, Peter and Andrew decided to leave the rest for a while and go out fishing in their boat. They fished all night but caught nothing, so they returned to the shore and began to rinse out their nets.

As they were busy doing this, Jesus came along, followed by a large crowd, and he stopped at the water's edge to speak to them.

Everyone wanted to get near to him so they pushed and jostled until Jesus was nearly in the water. He then asked Peter to get his boat and push it out into the water so that he could stand in it just off shore and continue to speak to the gathering of people.

As the sun got hotter towards noon, Jesus stopped preaching and the crowds dispersed. 'Let us go out a little further in the boat,' Jesus suggested to Peter, 'and try and catch some fish.'

'But master, we have fished all night already and caught nothing,' said Peter, who knew very well that mid-day was not the best time to go fishing.

Nevertheless, he did as Jesus said, sailed further out to sea and cast the nets overboard.

After a short time, when they tried to pull in the nets, they were so heavy with fish that they could not move them. They saw James and John in another boat and called them over to give them a hand. Together they were able to bring the catch on board. In fact they were able to completely fill both boats.

Peter was so surprised that he knelt before Jesus and asked him to forgive him for doubting.

The man with leprosy

Read: Mark 1 :40-45

There was once a man who had leprosy; he had ugly sores all over his body. People were afraid to go near him in case they caught the disease themselves, so the poor man was forced to live in a little shelter outside the city. His friends would bring him food and place it at the entrance to his hut before running away. When he did venture into the city people would shout, 'Leper! Leper!' or he himself would cry out, 'Unclean! Unclean!' He lived a very sad and lonely life.

One day Jesus came near the city. The man knew that Jesus had healed the sick in other places so he decided to look for him. As he made his way along the streets he wondered if he would ever manage to find Jesus. Then he saw the Lord surrounded by a crowd of people all wishing to speak to him or have him touch them so that they too might be healed.

When the leper approached, they began to shout at him to go away. But as he came close to Jesus he stretched out his hands saying, 'Lord, will you please make me well again. You can do it, if it is your will.'

Jesus did not chase the man away for he was not afraid of his sores. Instead, he touched the leper, placed his hands on his head and said, 'Of course I will. You are clean.' Immediately the sores were healed. The man thanked Jesus and praised God for healing him and went on his way rejoicing. Now that he was healthy again he was able to return to his own home and his family.

The man who couldn't walk

Read: Mark 2

The Lord Jesus was inside a house speaking to a crowd of people. Every room was crammed full and they jostled to get as near to him as possible. There were four men who were particularly keen to get close to Jesus. They had a friend who was crippled and they had to carry him on a mat. The man believed that God was angry with him and that this disease was some kind of punishment for his sins.

However, with the crowd of people in the house that day it seemed impossible for the men to get near enough to Jesus to speak to Him.

Then they had an idea. Outside there was a stair which led to the flat roof of the house. If only they could take their friend up there, they could make a hole in the roof and lower the man down to where Jesus was standing inside.

And that is what they did. They tied rope to each corner of the mat and carefully placed the man in front of Jesus while he was talking.

Jesus looked at the man and knew what he wanted without asking him. 'Don't be afraid,' he said, 'your sins are forgiven. Now, take up your bed and walk.'

Immediately the man did what he was told and he leapt up, praising and thanking God for such a miracle.

The people in the room could hardly believe their eyes. 'We have never seen anything like this before. How good and mighty the Lord is.'

Jesus raises a man from the dead

Read: Luke 7:11-17

Jesus and the disciples were visiting a city called Nain. As they approached the city walls a funeral procession came out of the gate. Among the mourners there was an old mother crying loudly. The body being carried out that day was her only son. She had already lost her husband and there would now be no one to look after her at home.

As Jesus watched the line of mourners, he felt sorry for the old woman and said to her, 'Do not cry.' As the woman dried her eyes and looked up, the Lord Jesus walked over and placed his hand on the young man's body. Then he said, 'Young man, wake up.'

The crowd were astonished when the man stirred, opened his eyes, sat up and began to talk. Then Jesus took him by the hand and led him to his mother. The woman threw her arms round her son and hugged him. She praised God and thanked Jesus as she returned home with her son.

Jesus calms the storm

Read: Luke 8:22-25

Jesus and the disciples returned once more to the seashore where crowds had gathered to hear him. As he had done before, he got into Peter's boat when the crowd crushed against him. When evening came, the Lord was very tired but still the people kept on coming. Eventually, Jesus said to Peter, 'Let's sail across to the other shore where we can have a rest.' Peter set sail with the other disciples and Jesus lay down at the back of the boat and fell fast asleep.

It was a quiet evening and at first the sea was calm but, when they were halfway across, the weather changed. The sky turned dark and the wind began to blow, whipping up large waves which began to beat against the side of the boat. As the storm worsened, the waves started to crash over on to the deck, and the disciples were afraid that the boat would sink.

Jesus was so tired that he slept through it all. The disciples went over to the Lord and woke him. 'Master, help us! We are drowning! Don't you care if we all drown?'

When Jesus woke up, he heard the roaring of the wind and the pounding of the waves but he was not afraid. 'Why are you afraid?' he asked. 'You know I won't let you drown.'

Then, standing up, he said to the wind and the sea, 'Be still!' Immediately all was calm. The disciples didn't say much after that except, 'How amazing! Even the wind and the sea obey him.'

The daughter of Jairus

Read: Luke 8:40-56

There once lived a man called Jairus, who was married with a daughter about twelve years old. The family lived in a house in Capernaum near the sea. One day, however, the little girl became ill. She was so weak that she was unable to eat or drink and it seemed that she was about to die. Her father and mother were very upset. Her father had heard that Jesus was in the area and decided to contact him to ask him to come and heal his daughter.

He ran into the street and hurried as fast as he could until he reached the seashore. There was a crowd there and in the middle Jesus stood talking to them. Jairus pushed his way through the crowd and fell on his knees before the Lord. 'Master, please come with me right now for my daughter is so sick she may die at any moment. If you will, you can make her whole again.'

Jairus showed Jesus the way to his home, but there were so many people wanting to see Jesus that it took a long time to get there.

Others stopped him on the way asking him to heal them, and that delayed him even more.

When they finally got near Jairus' house one of the servants came out to meet them, looking very sad. 'Your daughter has died. There is no need for Jesus to come to the house now, for there is nothing that can be done.'

Jesus turned to Jairus and said, 'Do not be afraid, only believe that I can help her.' When they went in to the house, Jesus told all the mourners to go outside, saying, 'Why are you all crying like this? The girl is not dead. She is only sleeping.'

Then he went into the room where the girl was lying. With him were her mother and father and three of his disciples. Taking the girl by the hand he said, 'Wake up, my child.' When the girl heard the voice of Jesus she opened her eyes and Jesus gave her to her mother. 'Now, give her something to eat,' said Jesus.

The boy who gave his lunch to Jesus

Read: John 6:1-14

Jesus and the disciples had gone over to the other side of the Sea of Galilee where they could rest for a while, but when they crossed over in Peter's boat, they found that the crowd had gone round to meet them. About five thousand people had gathered and, although Jesus was very tired, he didn't send them away. He continued to speak to them and heal the sick they had brought to him.

When evening came, there was nowhere for the people to go and no place to get anything to eat. The disciples said to Jesus, 'We had better send the people away so that they can go and get something to eat.' They were taken aback when Jesus said that they should find some food to give them. 'How can we do that? There are so many of them.'

'Go and see if anyone has any food,' said Jesus.

The disciples asked around until they found a little boy among the crowd who had brought with him five loaves of bread and two fish, but that was not nearly enough to feed the crowd. When they told Jesus that they had only found one lad with food, he told them, 'Bring the loaves and fish to me and ask all the people to sit down.'

Jesus then took the fish and the bread and asked God's blessing on the food that had been provided. He filled basket after basket and told them to share it out among the people.

Everyone had enough to eat that day. In fact there was so much, the disciples gathered up twelve baskets full of leftovers.

Jesus walks on the water

Read: Matthew 14:22-33

Jesus wanted to rest for a while so he told the disciples to go back on their own in the boat to the other side of Galilee. He would join them later. When they set out, the wind was against them, then the sea got rough and the wind began to rise as they rowed harder and harder against the storm. Soon they were sorry that the Lord Jesus was not with them to save them as he had done before. Although Jesus was still on the shore resting, he knew that they were struggling to reach the other side. The disciples continued trying to keep the boat on course but they were frightened.

What a shock they got when suddenly they saw a white shape looming in the darkness, walking towards them on top of the water. Then they heard the voice of Jesus, 'Do not be afraid, for it is I, the Lord.'

Peter cried out, 'Lord, is it really you? Let me come to you.'

Jesus replied, 'Come to me then.'

Peter climbed out of the boat and stepped on to the water. As long as he kept his eyes on Jesus he was able to walk towards him, but then the wind began to blow again and the water splashed round about him and Peter became afraid. He began to sink and shouted out, 'Lord, save me!'

Jesus was already by his side and reached out his hand to pull him up. Then together they climbed over into the boat to join the other disciples and the sea became calm again.

The man who wouldn't forgive

Read: Matthew 18:21-35

Jesus told a story to explain why we should learn to forgive those who have done wrong to us. There was once a king who lived in a palace with many servants. One of them owed the king a great deal of money and he demanded that he should repay him as soon as possible. But the man was unable to pay anything to him. 'Throw him in prison!' said the king to his guards. As they were about to take him away, however, the man fell on his knees, trembling before the king saying, 'Your majesty, please have pity on me!'

The man cried out, 'I don't have enough money just now but I shall pay back everything as soon as I am able to. Please don't send me to prison.'

It was really an empty promise for there was no way that he would be able to repay his debts. However, the king felt sorry for him and told him that he did not need to pay anything.

The servant left feeling very pleased with himself. As he walked home that day he met another one of the king's servants, in fact a man who actually owed him some money.

He didn't owe the servant nearly as much as he himself had owed the king but he took hold of him and shouted, 'What about that money you owe me? If you don't pay up, I'll have you put in prison.'

The man shook with fear and begged him, 'Give me some time and I will repay you as soon as I have the money. Please don't put me in prison.' But the first servant wouldn't hear of it and had him thrown into jail.

The king heard about the servant's actions and sent for him straightaway. 'You are so mean. I forgave you your debts so why could you not forgive the fellow servant who owed you money? For this, you can go to prison too.'

No matter how much he protested, this time the king showed him no mercy. Jesus concluded the story saying, 'So will my Father in heaven do to you if you do not forgive the wrongs that other men do to you.'

The Good Shepherd

Read: John 10

Jesus wanted to explain how much he cared for his followers and spoke about a shepherd and his sheep. A good shepherd, he told them, knows his sheep and they know his voice. He will watch over them to make sure that they do not get into danger, leading the way to green pastures along narrow and dangerous paths, while they follow on behind.

Once they reach the good grass he will watch and make sure that none of them wander away. But if one should stray, he would call it back and bring it to the fold to rejoin the others.

He would go out into the night if necessary and search, even if only one left the safety of the flock.

Whatever the danger, from rocky ground or wild animals, he would continue looking until he had found it.

Then Jesus explained that he is the good shepherd, who looks after his flock.

If ever any of his followers wandered away from him and found themselves in danger, he would not leave them alone but search for them and care for them, bringing them back into the fold of his love.

The Good Samaritan

Read: Luke 10

Jesus was speaking to a group of people one day when one of them asked, 'Who is my neighbour?' Instead of giving a straight answer, Jesus told a story to explain what he thought. A man set off on a long journey from Jerusalem to the city of Jericho. It was a difficult and dangerous road where travellers could be attacked and robbed. The man had not gone very far when robbers hiding in the bushes set upon him. They took his clothes, beat him, stole all his money and left him for dead.

As he lay bleeding, a priest who had been to the temple to pray passed nearby. But the priest did not want to get involved so he went on his way, leaving the man by the roadside, groaning.

A little later a Levite, a servant of a priest who knows all about the law, came along the road. He was a servant of God, surely he would help. But when he saw the fellow, he did not want to get involved either, and passed by on the other side of the road.

Then a Samaritan, a man from another country, not friendly with the Jewish people, came in sight. He got off his donkey, knelt down beside the injured man and bandaged his wounds.

Once he felt that the man was able to move, he helped him up, put him on his own donkey and took him to an inn where travellers could rest and spend the night. He put him into a room and made sure that he was safe and well throughout the night.

The next morning, the man was still not fit enough to travel. The Samaritan had to get on his way, so he left some money with the innkeeper saying, 'Take this money and look after this man until he is well. If he has to stay longer than I have paid for, let me know how much I owe you when I pass this way again.'

When he had finished the story Jesus asked, 'Which of these three men was the man's neighbour? The priest, the Levite or the Samaritan?' It was not a difficult question to answer and they replied, 'The Samaritan, of course.'

Jesus said, 'Now you must go and do the same.'

The Lost Son

Read: Luke 15

Jesus told another story to his followers to explain how much God cares even for those who decide to disobey him and go their own way: Once there was a rich man who lived in a beautiful big house. He had two sons and they lacked nothing. The elder son was an obedient boy who worked hard every day for his father, but the younger one was lazy and did not want to stay at home to work. Nevertheless, the father loved them both equally.

One day the younger son decided that he had had enough and wanted to leave home to make his living elsewhere. So he went to his father and asked him for his share of the family money.

'I am tired of living at home,' he said, 'I want to go out and see a bit of the world before I am too old to enjoy it.'

The father was very sad that his son was not happy to stay at home with the family, and reluctantly gave him his share and let him go on his way. Every day after that he kept a watch to see if his son would come back, but the son was having a wonderful time, spending his money enjoying himself in the big city.

There he was able to buy expensive clothes, eat delicious food and go to parties. Being so rich, he had plenty of friends who were eager to help him spend his money.

It seemed as if the money would last forever and he had a great time, without a care in the world.

All this time he was spending money but not earning anything to replace it. He soon found he had to start selling some of his clothes to get enough money to buy food.

When his friends realised that he had nothing to share with them, they left him. The young man had nothing so he had to go out into the streets and beg for a few crusts of bread. To add to his misery, there was a famine in the land and many other people were begging too. In despair, he asked a farmer to give him a job so he could earn enough for a bit of food.

He ended up looking after pigs, and was so hungry that he even wished he could have the scraps of food that the pigs were eating. He felt really sorry for himself and remembered what he had left behind in his father's house. He was ashamed to even consider returning home. But he got so desperate that he made up his mind that he would go back to ask his father to forgive him and see if he would take him back, even if only as one of his servants.

He set off for home, and when he was still a long way from the house, his father saw him coming along the road. When he realised that it was his son struggling up the road, he ran to him, threw his arms round him and kissed him.

The son couldn't believe what was happening and said, 'Father forgive me. If you are willing to take me back I shall become one of your servants.' But his father would not hear of it, and called his servants to clean him up and give him new clothes to wear. He even gave him a new ring for his finger and arranged to throw a party in celebration. 'Now my son has returned,' he said to everyone, 'I thought he was dead but he is alive. He was lost but now I have found him again.'

The raising of Lazarus

Read: John 11

Jesus often visited friends in a village near Jerusalem, called Bethany. In the house where he stayed, there were two sisters Mary, Martha and their brother Lazarus. They were delighted to have Jesus as their friend, and were pleased to welcome him and look after him when he was in the area. But one day, Lazarus fell ill and it looked as if he was going to die.

'If only Jesus was near,' said his sisters, 'He could heal Lazarus.' But Jesus was away in another part of the country, so they sent someone to look for him. When the man found Jesus he told him, 'Lazarus, whom you love, is sick and may die. Please come.'

But when Jesus managed to get to Bethany three days later, he was told that Lazarus had already died and had been buried. Mary and Martha were in mourning but Martha went out to meet Jesus. 'If only you had come earlier, master, our brother would not have died.'

'Believe in me,' Jesus said, 'and your brother shall live again.'

'Yes, Lord,' replied Martha, 'I believe that you are Christ, the Son of God.'

'Go and call Mary,' Jesus said.

Then Martha went back to the house to fetch her sister who was being comforted by friends. 'Mary, the master is here and is calling for you.' Mary went out to meet Jesus and the others followed behind. She cried and fell at his feet, saying, as Martha had done, 'Lord, if only you had come earlier, Lazarus would not have died.'

Then Jesus began to cry along with her and comforted her. Then he asked, 'Where is Lazarus buried?'

The mourners led the way to the cave where he had been put to rest. 'Take the stone away,' said Jesus.

'What do you want to do Lord?' asked Mary. 'He has already been dead four days...'

But the Lord Jesus said, 'Believe in me, Mary, and you will see how great God is.'

Some men rolled the stone away from the entrance to the cave and the people stood back to watch what Jesus was going to do. Jesus looked up to heaven and began to pray, then called out, 'Lazarus, come out!'

Suddenly they heard movement inside the cave and Lazarus came out, still bound up in the graveclothes he had been buried in. They jumped back in surprise and Jesus told them, 'Take off these graveclothes and let him go home.'

Mary and Martha were so happy that day as they walked home with Jesus and their brother.

Those who had witnessed the great miracle then knew who Jesus was, and believed that he was indeed the Son of God.

Let little children come to me

Read: Mark 10

One day a group of mothers were walking along a road with their children at their side. The older ones were being led by the hand and the smaller ones were being carried. They were happy because they were on their way to see the Lord Jesus. 'We want our children to know Jesus. If they meet him, they will never forget him.'

They also wanted to ask Jesus to lay his hands on the children and bless them.

When they came to Jesus he was alone with his disciples. When the disciples saw the mothers coming with their children, they stopped them and said, 'What do you want? Surely these children are too small and will not be able to understand what Jesus says. Children don't belong here, so don't bother Him.'

When the Lord saw what was happening he wasn't pleased with the disciples. He called the mothers and their children and said, 'Please come over to me.' And he said to his disciples, 'Let the children come to me. Don't keep them away, for the Kingdom of Heaven is for them too.'

The children stood beside him and he drew them close. Putting his arms around them he spoke to them and they knew that he loved them. Then Jesus laid his hands on their heads and blessed them.

Blind Bartimaeus

Read: Mark 10:46-52

A man was once sitting by the side of the road with his coat thrown over his shoulders. He looked as though he were asleep. Whenever he heard footsteps he would raise his head a little and listen. When they were very close he would hold out his hand and say, 'Please give me some money so that I can buy bread!'

Although he could hear footsteps he couldn't see the people. He could hear the swaying of the branches but he couldn't see the trees. Sometimes he would smell the sweet freshness of the flowers but he couldn't see their beautiful colours. All he knew was darkness. He had to feel his way from place to place, unable to see his way. There was no work for him to earn money, so he had to live by begging from people.

The beggar's name was Bartimaeus, and he had been blind for a very long time. There was no cure for his illness. However, he had heard about the Lord Jesus and thought he might be able to heal him. But Bartimaeus had never been near the Lord. Had he been able, he would have asked for his help, but he couldn't even look out for Jesus on the streets.

One day he was sitting by the road listening to the passing footsteps. Many people were on their way to Jerusalem for the feast of the Passover, as everyone wanted to join in the celebrations.

That particular day it seemed extra busy. There was such a large crowd that the ground shook under their feet. They were shouting and pushing each other so much that they sometimes bumped into Bartimaeus.

'Why are so many people passing all at once?' called Bartimaeus. 'What's going on?'

'Don't you know?' some of the people told him excitedly. 'Jesus is coming!'

Bartimaeus' heart began to pound in anticipation. Jesus was coming and perhaps he was close to him already. Maybe he would hear if Bartimaeus called him very loudly. So Bartimaeus began to call out, 'Jesus of Nazareth, have mercy on me!'

The people nearby were very angry with him. 'Be quiet,' they said. 'Do you think the Lord Jesus has time for you? He is going to Jerusalem to be made king.'

But Bartimaeus didn't pay any attention. They didn't know what it was like to be blind and sit all day in the darkness by the side of the road. He shouted all the louder, 'Jesus of Nazareth, have pity on me!'

Then, to his delight, a voice answered, 'Bring Bartimaeus to me. He is sitting over there by the roadside and is calling me.'

Then the people shouted, 'Bartimaeus, hurry up. Come over here !'

Struggling up, Bartimaeus threw off his coat and came to the Lord. With his arms outstretched he staggered through the crowd. 'What is it you want, Bartimaeus?' said a kind voice. 'What can I do for you?'

Bartimaeus replied, 'Lord, I want so much to be able to see.'

'Since you believe that I can heal you,' said the Lord, 'now you shall see.'

All at once Bartimaeus could see again. He saw green trees and a beautiful blue sky. He saw men and women and he saw the Lord Jesus, who had healed him! Falling on his knees, he thanked the Lord for having done as he asked.

When Jesus went on his way, Bartimaeus followed behind and danced with joy. Now he was a strong happy man who would never have to beg again because Jesus had touched him.

Hosanna to our King

Read: Matthew 21

Jesus was walking down the road which leads to Jerusalem with his disciples and other followers. They were wondering, 'Is he going to Jerusalem to become king?' This was what many of them wanted. There were enemies in the land, Romans, who treated the Jews very harshly. They believed that if the Lord Jesus were to become king, he would be able to help them defeat the Romans.

Suddenly Jesus stopped and spoke to two of the disciples, 'Do you see that village over there? On the outskirts you will find a young donkey tied by a rope. Untie it and bring it to me. If anyone asks what you are doing say, "The Lord needs it."'

The disciples wondered why the Lord would want a donkey. They thought he wanted to ride into Jerusalem. Perhaps he really did want to become king.

They walked towards the village, and there was the donkey, just as the Lord had said. It was tied near the door of one of the first houses. When they began to untie the rope, some men standing nearby asked, 'What are you going to do with the donkey?'

The disciples answered just as Jesus had told them, 'The Lord needs it.' Then the men let the donkey go.

Jesus' followers were pleased when they saw the disciples coming with the donkey. Now they knew what the Lord Jesus would do.

They took off their coats, laid them on the donkey's back and then helped the Lord to climb up. The disciples walked along beside him and the crowd followed, shouting, 'Here comes our King! Hosanna to our King!'

They pulled long palm branches from the trees and waved them like flags over his head. Some of them took off their coats and put them on the road so that the donkey could walk on them. Everyone was shouting and singing for joy. As they came closer to the city they shouted louder and louder, 'Hosanna! Hosanna!'

While all this was going on some men stood watching silently in the crowd. They were the priests and the Pharisees. They didn't join in because they didn't love Jesus. They were jealous of him because the people were so fond of him. Everyone was eager to hear Jesus preach and the priests didn't like it at all. 'The people must listen to us. We are much wiser than this man!'

When they saw Jesus riding into the city, and heard what the people were singing, they became very angry. They would have pulled him from the donkey if they thought the crowd would let them get away with it.

'Hosanna, our king!' the crowd continued to shout. The angry priests and Pharisees shouted back, 'Don't say this! He certainly isn't our king!'

Then the leaders came to Jesus and said, 'Master, tell your disciples they mustn't say these things.' But the Lord Jesus said nothing, for everything the crowd was saying was true. The Lord Jesus was a king, although he was not the kind of king the people were thinking about. He was no ordinary king, not one who would lead the people against the Romans in battle, but a King of Peace.

The people didn't understand, but thought that he would become their king immediately. This was why they were so excited. But Jesus knew many things would have to happen before he would be king. Many of the things would be dreadful and difficult. This was why he was sad as he rode through the streets of Jerusalem towards the great temple.

The people crowded around him, waiting for him to say, 'Now make me your king and we will fight our enemies together.' But he said nothing as he went into the temple that day. Jesus remained inside for a long time as the people waited outside.

Mary gives a gift to Jesus

Read: Mark 14:3-9 and Luke 7:36-38

Jesus was in Bethany, with Mary, Martha and Lazarus. He was sitting at the table and they were about to eat. Martha prepared the food. Lazarus sat close to the Lord. They were happy because Jesus was with them. Just as they were ready to eat, Mary walked in, holding a very expensive jar of perfume and she looked sad.

Mary knew that this would be the last time Jesus would be with them. He had told them that he would go to Jerusalem the next day and would not return. To show how much she loved him she wanted to do something special, so she had bought the most expensive jar of perfume she could afford. She stood behind Jesus and poured the precious oil over his head. Then she anointed his feet until the sweet smell filled the house.

Judas, one of the disciples, couldn't believe his eyes and complained, 'Why did she do that? We could have sold the perfume and given the money to the poor.'

Although Judas was a follower of Jesus, he was not an honest man. He probably wanted the money for himself. The other disciples complained too.

Jesus said, 'Be quiet, all of you. Why are you grumbling? Mary has done what is right. There will always be poor people but I will not always be with you. What Mary has done will never be forgotten.'

Then the disciples were quiet, for they felt ashamed of themselves. Judas however, was upset and left the house.

Judas betrays Jesus

Read: Matthew 26:1-5

Judas walked alone in the darkness of the night. He was angry with Jesus. Things weren't going the way that Judas had planned. Judas didn't care about the poor or about Jesus: all he was concerned about was whether or not he had fine clothes to wear or a large house in which to live. There were so many things he wanted. Now Judas was realising that he would get nothing at all.

He no longer wanted to be a disciple of Jesus. Instead, he made up his mind to go ahead with his plan to betray Jesus, even though the Lord had always been kind to him. Judas went to the enemies of the Lord, the priests and the Pharisees. 'What will you give me if I help you to arrest Jesus?' They promised him thirty pieces of silver. Judas wanted the money because he loved wealth above all other things. 'I will call you when you can catch him easily,' he said. 'I will stay with Jesus and pretend that I am still his friend.'

Stealing away into the darkness, he returned to the Lord Jesus and acted as if nothing had happened. But, unknown to him, Jesus knew all about it.

Jesus washes the disciples' feet

Read: Luke 22:7-13 and John 13

It was Passover in Jerusalem, and in every house tables were spread with wine, bread and meat. The feast would be celebrated in every home throughout the land. Jesus wanted to celebrate the Passover with His disciples for the last time. He called Peter and John and said, 'Go and make everything ready for the feast.' 'Which house do you want to go to?' asked the disciples.

'Go into the city. There you will see a man walking with a jug of water. Follow that man and go into the house which he enters. You must say to him, Where is the room where Jesus can celebrate Passover? Then he will show you a big room with tables and chairs, all ready for the feast.'

When the two disciples went to the city they found everything just as the Lord had told them. They met a man with a jug of water and followed him into a house. When they asked they were shown into a big room. Peter and John prepared the supper, placing the bread, wine and meat on the table. At the entrance to the room they placed a pitcher of water and a large basin so that the disciples could wash their dusty feet.

It was almost evening when the other disciples arrived. When they came into the room they each looked at the basin and wondered whether a servant would come and wash their feet. They were much too proud to wash each other's feet themselves, so they all sat down at the table with Jesus. He said, 'I want to celebrate this Passover with you as this is the last time I will be able to do it.' Then, without saying anything, he got up, poured some water into the basin, took a towel and then got down on his hands and knees in front of one of the disciples.

The disciples were shocked! Was Jesus going to do what they had all refused to do? Was he willing to be the servant and wash their feet? They were very ashamed of themselves. Peter felt worse than all the others and when Jesus came to wash his feet he drew them away saying, 'Lord, you shall not wash my feet!'

But Jesus looked at him and answered, 'If I do not wash your feet you cannot be my disciple. You do not belong to me!' Peter wanted very much to belong to the Lord and when he heard this he had to agree. Peter loved Jesus very much so he said, 'Lord, then wash not only my feet but also my hands and my head.'

Jesus washed the feet of all the disciples, including Judas who was going to betray him. When he had finished he put the basin away and came back to sit at the table. 'Do you understand why I have done this?' He asked. 'I have given you an example, for I wanted to teach you something. You mustn't quarrel about who is the most important. You must help each other and gladly do things for one another. Don't be afraid to be a servant. You will really be my disciples if you do these things.'

The disciples felt very ashamed of themselves but they had learned a lesson. They were sorry they had been so proud. But there was one who wasn't in the least bit sorry, for he no longer really belonged to the disciples – Judas.

The Last Supper

Read: Matthew 26

Jesus was sitting at the table with the disciples. 'Remember, this is the last time we will be together,' he said. 'It won't be long before my enemies come to take me away and then I must die. One of you here at the table will betray me and help my enemies.' The disciples looked surprised when he said this. Surely none of them would ever betray their master who had been with them for so long?

He had always been so good and kind to them, who could possibly be so wicked as to betray him? 'Who is it?' they asked.

John was sitting right next to Jesus and he whispered, 'Lord, who is it?'

And the Lord answered softly, 'The man to whom I give this piece of bread.' Then he gave the bread to Judas.

Judas also asked very boldly, 'Lord, is it I?'

'Yes, Judas!' answered the Lord Jesus. 'You are the one!'

The others didn't hear it but Judas was angry when he realised that Jesus knew all about him. 'You had better leave now and do as you have planned,' Jesus told him. He was going out to betray the Lord to his enemies.

After Judas had gone, Jesus was alone with the other disciples. They ate the bread and drank the wine, for they were celebrating the feast together.

'You must celebrate this feast, even after I am gone,' said the Lord. 'You must always keep this feast. Do you see how I am breaking this bread? My body will be broken in the same way for you. Do you see how I am pouring the wine? So will my blood be poured out for you. When you keep this feast, you must also eat bread and drink wine, for then you will remember how I died for you. You must never forget this.'

The Lord Jesus told his disciples many other things that evening as they sat together at the supper table. He told them that his enemies would come that very night to take him away. 'And all of you will leave,' he added. But the disciples shook their heads, 'No, we would never do a thing like that. We will never leave you!'

'Even if all the others leave you,' Peter protested, 'I will never leave you. I will fight for you and, if necessary, I will die for you!'

'Are you really willing to die for me, Peter?' asked the Lord. 'I tell you, this very night you will deny me three times. You will lie and say you are not my disciple at all. Before the cockerel crows tomorrow morning you will have denied me three times.'

Peter didn't believe a word of it and neither did the other disciples. But the Lord Jesus knew all that would happen that terrible night. Nevertheless, he told them not to be sad even although everything would seem to be going wrong, for all would turn out well in the end. He told them that he was going to die but that he would come back to life again. Later he would go to heaven and one day the disciples would go to be with him there.

Then they prayed together and the Lord Jesus prayed for his disciples and for all the people who would come to believe in him. When he had finished praying, he said, 'Come, let us go.' Then they went together into the darkness of the night.

The Garden of Gethsemane

Read: Matthew 26

Near the city of Jerusalem was a garden with many trees, called the Garden of Gethsemane. After the Last Supper the Lord Jesus walked sadly toward the garden with the disciples. His heart was sad, for he knew it wouldn't be long before men would come to take him prisoner. They would mock him and hurt him and then kill him. It was terrible, but it had to be. Jesus had never done anything wrong and didn't deserve to be punished like this. He didn't deserve to be punished at all.

The people themselves deserved to be punished for their sins, but Jesus had prayed, 'Father, I love them. Let me be punished in their place, so that those who believe may enter heaven.'

Now the time had come. The punishment would be hard and Jesus thought, 'I want to be alone. I want to pray to God to help me to bear it.'

When they reached the Garden, Jesus told his disciples, 'You had better stay here.' Peter, James and John went a little way with him into the Garden.

'I am very sad,' he told them. 'You must stay here, but don't go to sleep. Please stay awake and pray for me.' Then Jesus went a little further into the darkness of the Garden, where he fell on His knees and prayed, 'Father, I'm afraid and very sad because the time for the terrible punishment has come. I will do all that you want me to. Help me, Father, and make me strong.'

He stood up and went back to the disciples to speak with them about his sorrow, but they were all fast asleep. Waking them up, he said, 'Can't you stand by me for even an hour?'

But when Jesus left them again their heads sank and their eyes shut as they fell asleep again. Jesus knelt to pray once more. So great was his pain, big drops of sweat came to his forehead. 'Father, I will bear this punishment, but please help me!'

He told God everything and said, 'Father, help me to do all you want me to do.' Then an angel came down from heaven to comfort and strengthen him.

'Let the awful punishment come,' Jesus prayed. 'I am ready to bear it.'

Suddenly the stillness of the night was broken by the sound of voices. There were lanterns swaying in the darkness and men coming into the garden. The disciples woke up with a start when the noise came closer. They hurried over to Jesus. Judas was leading the men and showing them where to go.

Judas told them, 'I will show you which one he is and I will behave as though I am still his friend. The man whom I kiss on the cheek is Jesus.'

When Judas and the soldiers came close to the Lord, he said, 'Hello, Master!' and kissed Jesus.

Jesus asked him, 'Judas, are you betraying me with a kiss?'

Judas didn't say anything. As he stepped back, the Lord Jesus walked over to the soldiers and asked them, 'Who are you looking for?'

'Jesus,' they replied.

'I am he,' said the Lord Jesus.

Then a very strange thing happened.
All the soldiers fell to the ground as if they had been
knocked over – they were shocked and surprised.
Quickly they scrambled to their feet again and looked
at the Lord Jesus with awe. 'Was it possible that he was so
powerful as to knock us all down like that?'

'If you are looking for me do not hurt my disciples but let them
go on their way,' Jesus said. Then he held out his hands to them
and the soldiers grabbed him. Suddenly, Peter jumped forward,
wanting to fight for the Lord. 'Let him go!' he shouted. 'Let my
Master go!'

He had a sword which he swung wildly in the direction of the
soldiers. He hit one of them, cutting off his ear. 'Stop it, Peter!'
said the Lord 'Do not help me. The angels in heaven could also
help me if I asked them, for my Father would send a thousand
of them. I don't want that, however, for I must be taken.' Then
he went over to the wounded soldier and healed the ear.

Jesus' enemies, however, didn't treat him so kindly but
grabbed him, tied his hands tightly with rope as if he were a
dangerous criminal, and led him away. The frightened disciples
scattered in every direction as they ran from the Garden.

Jesus faces his enemies

Read: Matthew 26

In Jerusalem stood a beautiful big house belonging to the high priest, a man in charge of all the other priests. On the night of Jesus' betrayal, the high priest sat with other important men. They were all glad that Jesus had been taken prisoner. 'Now we have him we will never let him go again. He must die! After he is dead, the people won't listen to him and we will once again be the leaders.'

Jesus was brought in by the soldiers, his hands bound together. The leaders looked at him angrily, but Jesus stood calmly before them. The high priest asked Jesus many questions, but he did not reply. People accused him falsely but all that Jesus had done was to tell people about God and to heal the sick. The high priest asked Jesus, 'Don't you hear what people are saying about you? Have you nothing to say?' But still he remained silent. Then the priest asked, 'Are you the Son of God?'

This time Jesus answered, 'Yes, I am the Son of God. In a little while I shall go to heaven, but one day I shall come back to earth. You will all see me when I come on the clouds of heaven.'

The high priest shouted, 'How dare he say these things? He is not the Son of God. He is only the son of Joseph, the carpenter. This is blasphemy! He has mocked God!'

'He must die!' shouted the other men. 'Yes, he must die!'

Then they began to beat him. They spat on him and did many other terrible things to him. All the time Jesus did not complain or say a word to them.

Peter denies Jesus

Read: Matthew 26

When the soldiers took Jesus, the disciples ran away. They were afraid the soldiers would catch them too, so they hid in the darkness. Peter and John, however, quietly followed the soldiers, for they wanted to know where they were going to take the Lord. When they saw that he was being taken to the house of the high priest, Peter didn't want to go any further.

But John knew the servant girl who worked for the high priest so he knocked at the door and asked, 'May I come in with this friend of mine?' The girl let them in, and so it was that Peter got into the house where Jesus was being held.

Peter was very afraid, for he thought, 'This is dangerous. This is the house of the enemy. I hope they don't find out I'm a disciple of the Lord Jesus and arrest me too. Look how that servant girl stares at me.'

Walking past the girl, he went into the inner court. Some soldiers were sitting round a blazing fire. Peter walked over to the fire to warm himself and from there he saw Jesus, standing bound in front of the priests in the next room. When the servant girl walked over to the fire, she looked at Peter and asked, 'Aren't you one of the disciples of Jesus?' Peter was startled. 'No, not me. I don't even know the man!' Peter became even more afraid than before and walked towards the door. When he got there he found the servant girl talking with some men. She said to the others, 'This man also belongs to Jesus!'

Peter was very afraid. 'No, that is not true,' he said. 'I don't know that man at all.'

Peter didn't know what to do, so he went back to the soldiers around the fire. He knew how Jesus was being treated. 'If they catch me,' he thought, 'they'll beat me like that too.'

All at once, a soldier asked, 'Aren't you one of his disciples?'

'No!' shouted Peter, swearing. 'It's a lie. I don't even know the man.'

All of a sudden a cockerel crowed. When Peter heard it he remembered what the Lord had said, 'Before the cockerel crows, you will have denied me three times.' Then he went outside and sobbed loudly.

'Oh Master, what wrong I have done. Dear Lord Jesus, please forgive me.'

Pilate the Roman Ruler

Read: Matthew 27

The night had passed and Jesus was still with the Jewish leaders. They wanted to kill him but couldn't. The Romans ruled the land so the priests had to speak to them. The most important Roman in Israel was Pilate so the high priest and the others took Jesus to him. They wanted to ask him if they might kill Jesus. Many people went with them and more joined them in the street. Pilate lived in a fine palace and when he saw the crowd coming with Jesus, he went outdoors. 'Why do you bring this man to me?' he asked. 'He must die!' they shouted. 'He has done much evil.'

'What did he do?' asked Pilate.

They told him all sorts of lies, but Jesus said nothing. Pilate looked at the prisoner, standing there quietly, and saw that he didn't even seem angry with all the lies.

When Pilate spoke to Jesus he felt sure that he had done nothing wrong, but he was afraid to let Jesus go because of the crowd outside. Then he had an idea. He sent his soldiers to the prison where the murderers were kept and they brought a man called Barabbas to the palace to stand beside Jesus.

'As is the custom on Passover day,' said Pilate, 'one of these men may go free and you may choose which one. Whom shall I free, Barabbas or Jesus?' Pilate was sure that they would choose a good man like Jesus rather than Barabbas, a murderer.

But he didn't know how angry the men were with Jesus. He was very surprised when they all shouted, 'Let Barabbas go!'

Pilate was shocked. 'What shall I do with Jesus?' he asked. 'Crucify him!' shouted the priests. 'He must die!'

The people shouted too, 'Yes, he must die! Crucify him!'

Jesus heard it. He had done nothing wrong, but had healed their sick and blessed their children. They had even wanted to make him king not so long ago. Now they mocked him as he stood helpless, his hands tied with rope. They shouted all the louder. 'Away with him! Crucify him, and let Barabbas go!'

Pilate then freed Barabbas because he was afraid of the people, but he tried once more to keep Jesus from the cross. Taking Jesus inside, he ordered the soldiers to pull off his clothes and whip him on the back. Then they dressed him in an old robe and began to tease him. They made a crown of thorns and placed it on his head as they laughed. 'What a fine king you are.'

Jesus said nothing but let them do as they pleased. Then Pilate took Jesus outside once again and placed him before the people. He was sure they would feel sorry for him, when they saw how sick and tired he looked.

But the priests had no pity and neither did the crowd. They shouted again, 'Away with him. Crucify him!'

They shouted so hard and for such a long time, that Pilate became afraid of them. 'All right,' he said. 'Take him and do what you want with him.'

The soldiers then took Jesus away to be crucified.

Golgotha

Read: Matthew 27, Mark 15:21, John 19:25-27

When the soldiers led Jesus away to be crucified they took a cross and laid it on his shoulders. The cross was made of two heavy pieces of wood nailed together and Jesus had to carry it to the place of execution. The soldiers walked in front as they led him through the streets of Jerusalem. Many people went along shouting and screaming at him as they elbowed their way past each other.

The Lord had suffered a lot already and was so tired that he could hardly carry the heavy cross on his shoulders. Suddenly he fell down on the road, with the cross lying across his back.

'Get up!' shouted the soldiers. 'Pick up that cross!'

But Jesus couldn't carry it any further so the soldiers grabbed a man called Simon. 'Come here. Carry the cross for that man.'

The soldiers pulled Jesus along with them and Simon followed behind, carrying the cross. They left Jerusalem and came to the fields outside the city, where there was a bare sandy hill called Golgotha. Here the soldiers drove nails through his hands and feet and then stood the cross upright in the ground. Still Jesus wasn't angry with the men. He asked God not to punish them for their cruelty. 'Father, forgive them,' he said, ' for they do not know what they are doing.'

Two other crosses were placed next to him. On them were two criminals. The people stood and watched along with the priests and the Pharisees. 'Look at him,' they shouted. 'He said he was the Son of God. Why doesn't God help him now? Why doesn't he come down from the cross?'

The people mocked Jesus as he hung on that awful cross. Even the soldiers mocked him and so did one of the criminals hanging on the cross next to him. 'If you are the Son of God, why don't you save yourself and us?' But the other criminal said, 'Be quiet. We deserve to die but this man has done nothing wrong.' Then, turning towards Jesus, he said, 'Lord, remember me when you enter your Kingdom.' The Lord replied, 'Today you will be with me in Paradise.'

Not everyone standing near the cross was his enemy. Mary, the mother of Jesus, was there with John, one of the disciples. Mary was very sad to see how her son had to suffer. She could do nothing and soon Jesus would be dead. Who would take care of her then? When Jesus saw his mother, he pitied her and, looking towards John, said to her, 'Woman, behold your son.' And to John he said, 'Behold your mother.' John knew what Jesus meant. He took Mary to his home and looked after her from that time on.

Jesus hung on the cross for a long time. It was noon and the sun was high in the sky, beating down on his head. Suddenly the sun disappeared, although it wasn't evening. It grew very dark and everyone around the cross became afraid. Jesus felt as though his Father in heaven wanted nothing more to do with him. It was dark for three long hours then Jesus cried out, 'My God, my God, why have you left me alone?'

Then the darkness lifted. The punishment that Jesus had to take was almost over. He cried out for something to drink. 'I am thirsty,' he groaned. A man came with a long stick and on the end was a sponge. He wet the sponge with vinegar and held it up to the lips of Jesus. Jesus cried out, 'It is finished!' then bowed his head and died. His great work was done. The way to heaven was open for all who would trust in him.

Jesus is buried

Read: Matthew 27

Jesus was dead but his body was left on the cross until evening when his friends came and carefully lifted him down. They had fine linen clothes in which to wrap his body, with sweet-smelling spices tucked into the folds. Then they reverently carried him to a nearby garden where there was a cave cut into the rock. They put him inside and rolled a large stone across the entrance.

The followers of Jesus were in mourning. 'Now the Lord Jesus is dead, he can never talk to us again. He can never bless us or make us happy anymore. We thought we could be happy with him, but everything went wrong!'

They had completely forgotten Jesus' words, 'I shall die, but shall come back to life again. After three days I shall rise from the grave!'

Had they remembered his words, they wouldn't have been sad at all. But the enemies of the Lord Jesus hadn't forgotten his words.

The priests and the Pharisees sent soldiers to the grave and told them to watch it carefully. 'Make sure nothing happens to it,' they told the soldiers. 'The grave must stay closed and Jesus must remain inside.'

The Resurrection

Read: Matthew 28

It was early morning, three days after Jesus' death. The soldiers still stood guard over the grave to make sure nothing happened. Suddenly the ground began to shake and the grave burst open. An angel in a white robe stood at the entrance and rolled the stone away. The terrified soldiers fainted - collapsing in a heap.

At that time, the women who had helped to bury Jesus were walking towards the grave to place more sweet-smelling spices in the grave clothes. When they came to the garden they remembered the heavy stone that was placed at the opening of the grave and wondered, 'Who will help us roll it away?'

When they looked at the grave, they were surprised to see that the stone had already been pushed aside. One of the women, Mary Magdalene, left the others and ran back to the city to tell the disciples what had happened. The others went inside the cave. They got a fright when they saw two angels standing over the grave clothes.

But the angels said, 'Do not be afraid. You are seeking Jesus who was crucified. He is not here, for he is risen. Come, see the place where he lay. Don't you remember what the Lord told you? "I will die, but after three days I will rise from the grave."'

Then they remembered and were filled with joy. 'Go quickly and tell the disciples,' the angels said, 'and don't forget Peter!'

They hurried down the road when who did they meet but the Lord. He was alive and standing in front of them.

The women fell down on their knees before him, took hold of his feet and cried for joy.

Jesus said, 'Go, tell my disciples that they may also see me.'

And then the women were alone again, for Jesus was suddenly gone. But now they knew for certain that he was alive again. They had seen him and had heard his voice.

Quickly they went back to the city to look for the disciples. They laughed and shouted, 'The Lord Jesus has risen from the dead!'

But the disciples didn't believe them and shook their heads sadly. 'You must have been dreaming,' they said.

Mary Magdalene

Read: John 20:1-18

Mary Magdalene stood near the grave, crying. She did not know that Jesus had risen from the dead. She had run off to tell the disciples that the stone had been rolled away. While she was gone, the other women had seen Jesus. Mary still thought his body had been taken. She was beside herself with grief as she bent down and looked inside the dark cave.

Then she saw the two men sitting there, dressed in white robes, in the place where Jesus had been. She didn't realise that they were angels.

'Woman, why are you crying?' one angel asked.

Mary sobbed, 'Because they took away my Lord and I do not know where they have laid him.' Then she turned round and saw a man standing by her. It was the Lord, but Mary could not see, for tears were blinding her eyes.

The Lord asked, 'Woman, why are you crying? Who are you looking for?'

Mary still did not see that it was the Lord, but thought it was the gardener. She cried, 'Sir, did you take him away? Please, tell me where you have laid him.'

Jesus said simply, 'Mary.' At once Mary recognised his voice.

'Master! Dear Master!' she cried. She wanted to hold him tightly and never let him go again. But the Lord said, 'Do not touch me, for I cannot always stay here. I am going to my Father in heaven again. Go and tell my disciples these things.' Then he disappeared.

Mary was no longer sad for her Master was on earth again. She ran back to the disciples and called out, 'I have seen the Lord!' and told them everything she had seen and heard. But the disciples still could not believe it.

The road to Emmaus

Read: Luke 24

That same day two men were walking down the road from Jerusalem to a small town called Emmaus, where they lived. They were talking about the Lord Jesus. They said, 'What a pity it is that he died. We were sure that he would be king. We thought that he was the Saviour, the Son of God, but he couldn't have been or he wouldn't have been allowed to die.'

'And what about the stories told by the women in Jerusalem?' one asked the other. 'Can you believe them? They said that he rose from the grave but how can that be? If it is true, then he must be the Son of God. But why did he have to die in the first place?'

It was all a mystery to them and they shook their heads in disbelief.

Then a man began to walk along with them. It was the Lord Jesus, but they did not realise it. He asked them, 'What are you talking about and why are you looking so sad?'

'Don't you know what has happened in Jerusalem?' they replied. 'What happened?' asked the stranger.

'Don't you know what happened to the Lord Jesus?' they asked. 'You have heard about him surely. He was always good and kind. He healed the sick, gave sight to the blind and did many other miracles. But they crucified him and now he is dead.

We thought he was the Saviour. He has been dead for three days, yet today we heard that some women in Jerusalem say that he is alive again.' They thought that the man would agree with them and say, 'No, that cannot be true.' But he said, 'How foolish you are. Why don't you believe it, for it is true. Jesus really has risen and now you ask why he died?'

The man told them many other things and as they listened their sadness left them. Now they understood, and were certain that he was alive.

They wanted to keep on talking to the man but, when they reached their home, they had to stop. 'Won't you stay with us? It is already evening. Soon it will be dark and you cannot travel in the night.'

The man agreed to stay and went into their house with them. He sat down with them at the table to eat. Then he prayed and, taking the bread from the table, he broke it and gave a piece to each of them.

Suddenly they recognised him. But all at once Jesus disappeared from their midst. 'We should have known,' they said, 'Didn't our hearts feel warm as we talked with him on the road?'

They hurried back to Jerusalem to tell the disciples what had happened. When they got there, they found that the disciples had locked the door, for they were afraid of the Jewish leaders. But when the two men knocked, the door was opened for them.

Before they could tell their wonderful news, the disciples called out, 'The Lord Jesus has really risen. Peter has seen him.'

'Yes,' said the two, 'we also saw him.'

While they were still busy talking, someone else suddenly stood before them. How had he got in, for the door was locked and the windows were tightly closed? They were startled and a little afraid, but he said, 'Don't be afraid, for it is I. Come and see: touch me and look at me.'

He showed them his hands and feet with the marks of the nails still on them. He even asked them for something to eat. Then they believed that it was really the Lord. He sat with them at the table just as before and they were able to talk to him.

When he left them again no one was sad, for they knew for certain that he was alive and that he was indeed the Saviour.

At the seashore

Read: John 21

Before he left, Jesus told his disciples to meet him by the sea of Galilee. Seven of them, including Peter, walked by the shore watching out for him. Peter's boat was tied up nearby. They waited a while but there was no sign of the Lord. Peter suggested that they should go fishing. It was almost evening and they fished through the night but by morning had caught nothing.

Then over the water they heard a voice calling them. A man was standing on the beach but it was still quite dark so they weren't sure who it was. 'Have you caught anything?' the man called. 'No,' they replied. 'Try casting the net on the other side of the boat,' the stranger suggested 'and you will catch fish.'

They did as they were asked and sailed further out. When they tried to pull the net out of the water they couldn't move it because it was so full of fish. The man had been right, but who could he be? John turned to Peter and said, 'It is the Lord.' Peter jumped into the water and began to wade towards Jesus. Jesus was sitting cooking fish over a fire. By the time the rest got there, he had everything ready for them. Jesus said, 'Bring a few of the fish you have just caught.'

When Peter pulled the net up on to the beach he was amazed to find 153 fish caught in the net. Even though there were so many fish, the net was not damaged at all. The Lord sat with his disciples in a circle round the fire. He took bread and fish and passed it to them as they talked together.

During the meal, however, Peter had many thoughts about the time he had denied the Lord before his death. Three times he had said that he was not one of his disciples. When they had finished their breakfast, the Lord Jesus said to Peter, 'Do you love me more than the other disciples?'

Peter was startled. He had once said that he loved the Lord Jesus more than the others. 'Even if all of them leave you,' he had said, 'I will never leave you. I am willing to die for you.'

Peter replied, 'Yes, Lord. You know that I love you.'

The Lord Jesus said, 'Then feed my lambs.'

For a few minutes no one said anything, then Jesus asked him again, 'Peter, do you love me?'

Peter was sad. Did Jesus not believe him? 'Lord, you know that I love you.'

The Lord said, 'Tend my sheep.' Then Jesus asked for the third time, 'Peter, do you love me?'

Three times Peter had lied and said that he did not know the Lord Jesus. Now he was asked three times to say whether he loved the Lord. Peter sobbed it out, 'Lord, you know all things. You know also that I love you.'

The Lord Jesus replied, 'Feed my sheep. When you were young you did what you liked to do, but when you are old others will take you where you do not want to go. Follow me.'

Then Peter knew that the Lord had forgiven him and he now wished to be his servant, helping those who put their trust in him - the 'sheep' and 'lambs' that he spoke about.

Jesus goes to heaven

Read: Acts 1

After Jesus had risen from the grave he stayed on earth for a short time. He had finished all that he had to do on earth and it was time for him to go back to heaven. Before this, he met once more in Jerusalem with the disciples, except the traitor Judas, who was dead. They listened to what he had to say. They knew that it would be the last time they would be with him on earth.

Jesus told them that soon they would begin the work that he had taught them to do. They must go into all the world to tell people everywhere about him. It would be wonderful work but dangerous and difficult. However, he promised that in all their difficulties he would help them and care for them. 'I will not leave you alone. I will send someone to be with you, the Holy Spirit, who will make you wise and strong. He will also tell you what to do, so wait in Jerusalem until he comes.'

When Jesus had told the disciples everything they needed to know, he walked with them to the Mount of Olives. When they reached the top he raised his hands and blessed them as he went up to heaven. The disciples stayed there gazing up to heaven. Suddenly two angels stood by them and said, 'Why are you looking up to heaven? Jesus has not gone away forever. One day he will return just as you saw him go away.'

When they heard this they went home rejoicing, and waited in Jerusalem for the coming of the Holy Spirit as he had told them to do.

The coming of the Holy Spirit

Read: Acts 2

It was the Day of Pentecost, a Jewish feast, when people from all over the country flocked to Jerusalem to celebrate and worship. The disciples gathered in a room near the temple. Without warning there was a strange noise, like a wind blowing. Some of the crowd nearby heard it too and ran over towards the house.

When they got to the room they were amazed to see a group of men praying and praising God. What looked like flames seemed to be hovering above their heads but it did not burn them.

The disciples shouted for joy, for the Holy Spirit had come into their hearts just as Jesus had promised.

The people watching said, 'What is going on here? What does all this mean?' There were some who started to laugh saying, 'We know what it means. They have been drinking too much, that is why they are acting so strangely.'

Peter stood up to speak. 'No, we are not drunk. It is far too early in the day for that! What you see was foretold long ago by the prophet Joel. What you see happening was promised to us by Jesus of Nazareth, whose miracles you witnessed. He was put to death by lawless men but God raised him from the dead and he has now returned to be with his father in heaven. He has poured out the Holy Spirit on us and this is what you see and hear in this room.'

The people were greatly touched by Peter's words. 'What can we do?'

Peter said, 'You must ask God to forgive you for what you have done wrong, believe in Jesus Christ and be baptised. Then you also will receive the gift of the Holy Spirit.'

It was certainly a Pentecost to remember that day in Jerusalem, for about three thousand people believed and came to the disciples to be baptised in the name of the Lord Jesus.

The man who was born lame

Read: Acts 3

Once there was a man who sat by the temple begging. He was born with a disease in his legs and had never been able to walk. As a result he could not work, and depended on others to give him money to live on. When people walked past he would plead with them, 'Please spare me some money to buy bread.'

One afternoon he sat by the temple as usual, when Peter and John came along. When he held out his hand for some money Peter said, 'I have no money to give you, but I can give you what I have.' Then, to the man's surprise Peter said, 'In the name of Jesus Christ of Nazareth, get up and walk.' Then he took him by the hand and helped him stand up. His feet and ankles grew strong and he was able to walk just like everyone else.

The beggar laughed and shouted with joy, leaping around and praising God. 'I can walk. I am not a cripple, for the Lord has healed me.' He told everyone as he went into the temple with Peter and John. Everyone wondered what it was all about.

'Isn't that the crippled man who sat and begged by the temple door?' They all came and stood around Peter and John.

Peter said to them, 'Do not look at us like that, for we did not make this man well. The Lord Jesus has done this, the same person whom you crucified. But he is not dead. He has risen from the grave and now sits with his Father in heaven.'

When the priests in the temple heard what Peter was saying, they did not like it at all and told the temple guards to arrest Peter and John. The two men were thrown into prison. But many people became believers that day when they heard what Peter had to say.

The next morning the soldiers came back and brought them to the priests. 'In whose name and with what power did you heal that man?'

Peter and John then told them about Jesus and how he had sent the Holy Spirit to give them power to do things in his name. The priests were concerned that the news about Jesus would spread. They told Peter and John, 'You must not talk about Jesus any more. If you do you will be punished.'

But Peter and John replied, 'God has told us to preach and that is what we must do. We shall obey him and we must speak about all the things that we have seen and heard.'

The priests were afraid of what the people might say if they punished these good men. So they set them free and the disciples rejoiced, praising God for what he had done for them.

Peter in Prison

Read: Acts 12

The followers of Jesus continued to preach everywhere and many people were healed by the power of the Holy Spirit. The high priest was very angry when he heard what was happening, and the other leaders were jealous of the apostles. They wanted to put a stop to it so they had the men arrested and thrown into prison.

Peter, in particular, had caused them a lot of trouble for many years, and they wanted to silence him for good. He was sent to a secure prison before his trial and probable execution. The outer and inner doors were securely locked.

The soldiers were afraid that he might escape so he was guarded night and day by two men. There was a chain on each arm fastened to the arms of the soldiers. If he tried to get up in the middle of the night, they would waken at once. But Peter was not afraid for he trusted the Lord.

As he lay quietly sleeping in prison his friends, in a house nearby, were praying for him through the night. 'Lord, please help Peter. We cannot do anything for him now, but you can do all things.'

During the night, when the guards had dozed off, an angel came and stood close to Peter. He shook Peter awake and said, 'Get up quickly!' He stood up and as he did so, the chains dropped off his arms without disturbing the soldiers.

'Now put on your shoes and coat and follow me,' the angel continued. As he followed, the prison doors opened and they walked past the guards as if they were invisible.

Peter thought he was dreaming but realised that he was really outside when the angel led him along the street towards his friends' house. Then the angel disappeared.

Peter knocked on the door and startled the people inside. They were still praying for him and wondered who it could be at the door in the middle of the night. Perhaps the soldiers were coming to take them to prison as well!

Rhoda, the servant girl, went to answer the door. 'Who is there?' she asked cautiously.

'Don't be afraid, open the door,' said a voice.

When she recognised Peter's voice, she was so excited that she forgot to open the door and ran back to tell the others. 'Peter is standing at the door! Peter is here again!'

'You must be mistaken,' they said.

'No, it is Peter,' said the girl. 'Listen, there he is knocking again.'

They all hurried to the door and opened it. 'Peter, is it really you? How did you get out of prison?' They all talked at once as they crowded around him.

Peter asked them to be quiet, so that he could tell them how the Lord had answered their prayers. After spending a short time with them Peter escaped, in case the soldiers were searching for him. He moved away from the area but wherever he went he continued to preach about the Lord Jesus.

Paul's Travels

Read: Acts 9

One of the Jewish leaders who persecuted Christians was a man called Paul. He felt sure that it was his duty to round up those who believed in Jesus and put them in prison. Jesus of Nazareth had said that he was the Son of God, but Paul believed that he was an imposter who deserved to be put to death for blasphemy.

Even after his death, his disciples were spreading lies that God had raised him from the dead – they had to be stopped!

Paul was on his way to Damascus to arrest more Christians and have them brought back to Jerusalem. As he was nearing the city, a bright light suddenly flashed from heaven. He was so startled that he covered his eyes with his hands and fell to the ground. Then he heard a voice calling out his name, 'Why do you want to hurt me?'

Paul asked in a trembling voice, 'Who are you, Lord?'

The voice said, 'I am Jesus whom you want to hurt. Get up and go to the city. There I will tell you what you are to do.'

The bright light disappeared but, when Paul stood up and opened his eyes, he found to his horror that he could not see. His servants held him by the hand and took him to Damascus where they led him to a house. He was still blind and could neither eat nor drink. He couldn't help thinking about what had happened and he could not get that voice out of his head.

Three days later an old man called Ananias, who was a follower of Jesus, came to see him. God had told him to go to Paul and pray that he would get his sight back again. Ananias wasn't very sure about this because he had heard a lot about the man who had been arresting Christians. But the message from the Lord was clear, so he did what he was told.

Sure enough, when he reached the house that he had been told to visit, there was Paul. He placed his hands on Paul's head and said, 'Brother, the Lord Jesus who spoke to you on the road has sent me to you. You will be able to see again and will be filled with the Holy Spirit so that you can become one of his servants.'

Then it seemed to Paul as if dark scales fell from his eyes and he was able to see again. He stood up and said, 'Now I would like to be baptised, for I also want to be a disciple of the Lord Jesus.'

He stayed in Damascus for a few more days and began to tell others that Jesus was the Son of God. The people were very surprised and said, 'Isn't that Paul who came here to arrest the followers of Jesus and put them in prison? Now he is a disciple himself!'

The Jewish leaders were taken aback by what had happened to Paul. They were annoyed that he was now going around saying that Jesus was the Son of God. It was too dangerous to allow him to continue, so they plotted to kill him. They put spies at the gates of the city to look out for him, but he managed to escape when his friends lowered him in a basket over the wall during the night. After he escaped from Damascus he went first to Jerusalem and then to other towns and cities to preach and to meet believers. Some of the Christians didn't trust him at first, thinking that it might be a trick to arrest them and put them in prison. But when they heard what he had to say, and realised that the Jewish leaders were plotting to kill him, they knew that Paul had indeed become a disciple of the Lord Jesus.

Paul travelled everywhere to preach the gospel, not only in Israel, but to many other countries of the world.

Into all the World

Read: Acts 16

Jesus told the disciples to go into the world and preach the gospel. As they travelled around meeting people their work was not always easy. It was often dangerous because many people opposed them, and some wanted to kill them but, with the power of the Holy Spirit, they were not afraid. No matter how difficult it was they continued to tell people about Jesus wherever they went.

Paul travelled furthest of all, over land and sea. Once he and his friend Silas found themselves in a city called Philippi where there were leaders who did not want to hear about the Lord Jesus. They had the two men arrested and whipped before throwing them into prison along with thieves and murderers. 'Be sure to put these men in a safe place! They say they are servants of God but they are nothing of the kind,' they told the jailor. To make sure they could not escape, the man put them into the deepest cell in the prison, chained them to blocks of wood and guarded them carefully.

Paul and Silas had every right to feel miserable in the darkness, as their backs stung from the beating and the chains rubbed against their flesh. Instead, they said to each other, 'God sees us in this dark cell and he will take care of us. The Lord Jesus suffered much for us. Now we may suffer for him.' Such was their inner strength and peace that they even sang a hymn in the middle of the night. The jailor and the other prisoners heard them, and wondered what they had to sing about.

While they were singing at the top of their voices, suddenly there was a powerful earthquake. The ground shook, the walls of the prison cracked and burst open and the chains which shackled Paul and Silas fell off. There was nothing to stop them escaping. The jailor had fallen asleep but was wakened by the noise of the earthquake. He panicked when he stood up and realised that the walls and doors had burst open. If all the prisoners had escaped, he knew that his life was not worth living. He was about to kill himself when Paul shouted out, 'Do not harm yourself. We are all still here.'

The jailor could hardly believe his ears and rushed for a lamp. Sure enough, he found that Paul and Silas were still in the prison, although there were no chains attached to them. If they had been the evil men that the leaders said they were, why hadn't they escaped? The jailor fell down before Paul and Silas and asked them, 'Sirs, help me too! What must I do to be saved?'

Paul answered, 'Believe in the Lord Jesus Christ and you and your household will be saved.'

Paul and Silas spoke about Jesus to the jailor and he took them to his house, where he washed their wounds and gave them food and drink. Others in his house wanted to hear the message of the gospel and they too believed in the Lord. Later they were all baptised and became followers. The next morning Paul and Silas were set free by the magistrate. They went on their way again to other cities and countries throughout the world to tell people about the Lord Jesus.

For the rest of his life Paul was a faithful servant of the Lord Jesus. There were always other believers to continue the work which the first disciples had started. Many churches were set up throughout the world. The numbers grew each year as news spread about the gospel of Jesus Christ, and lives were changed by the power of the Holy Spirit.

The story of the ten young women

Read: Matthew 25

Before Jesus ascended to heaven he told his disciples that one day he would return. It will be a very special day, but no one knows exactly when it will be. Certainly the whole world will be aware of it when it does come. On that day the whole world will see Jesus and know that he is the King of heaven and earth. Everyone who believes in him will celebrate his coming again.

Jesus told his followers that they should watch and pray for this special day. His kingdom will be set up on earth for all those who have put their trust in him. It will be a kingdom where there will be no crime and no wars nor arguments.

Jesus warned that there would be those who would not be happy to see that day, for they have not prepared for it, nor trusted Jesus to forgive them their sins. He told a story to illustrate what would happen when he comes back again. 'Once there were ten young women dressed in their finest clothes and each one carrying an oil lamp. Two of their friends were about to be married and there was to be a wedding party for them. The girls were waiting for the bridegroom to come along the road so that they could walk together to the feast. But the road was dark and quiet and there was no sign of the bridegroom, so the girls sat down. They were tired and soon fell asleep, not realising that the oil in their lamps was nearly finished and that the lights were getting dim.

Suddenly there was the sound of music in the distance and they saw lights swaying back and forth in the darkness. Voices shouted, 'The bridegroom is coming. Come and meet him.' But when the girls grabbed their lamps to run and meet him, they realised that they had gone out.

Five of the girls had planned ahead and had brought extra oil to top up their lamps. However, the other five did not bother to carry oil with them and wanted to borrow from their friends. 'Please give us a little oil,' they begged. 'Our lamps are almost out.' Their friends could not help them for, if they did so, they would not have enough for themselves. So the five girls ran away as fast as they could to buy some oil while their friends led the way to the feast.

They found that the room was filled with laughter and music and delicious food was on all the tables. The five wise girls sat down at the table with all the other guests and the doors were closed as the feast began.

A little later there was a knock at the door. 'Open the door please. We have now got oil for our lamps and we would like to join the feast.' The bridegroom heard them knocking and told them, 'I do not know you. You do not belong to our group of friends, for they have already come inside with us.'

So the five wise girls were allowed to celebrate the wedding supper, but the five foolish girls had to stay outside in the darkness.'

After Jesus told that story he added, 'Be watchful of your faith, for you must be ready like the girls in the story. You do not know when I will come back but you must be ready for that great day.'

Servants of Jesus

Read: Matthew 25:14-30

Jesus told a story about what it meant to be one of his servants: Once there was a rich man who lived in a big house with many servants . He was a merchant who bought and sold all kinds of things, and each year he became wealthier and wealthier. One day he had to go abroad and it would be a long time before he returned.

He wanted to keep his business going during his absence so he called some of his servants to his office. First he called in his best servant and giving him five bags of money, told him, 'Do the best you can with this money and see what you can earn for me.'

Then he called a second servant and gave him two bags of money with the same instructions. Finally, he called in a third servant and gave him one bag to see what he could make out of it. They were all told to work as hard as possible and do the best they could until he returned home.

The first servant began to work hard, buying and selling goods and making a lot of money in the process. After a while he had doubled the money and had ten bags to show for his efforts. The second servant did the best he could but was unable to get as much business as the first. Nevertheless, he too was able to earn double what he had been given in the first place and now had four bags to return to his master. Every day the first two servants waited for their master to return to show him what they had been able to do with his money. But the third servant did not work hard to earn money from the amount he was given. He knew very well that he could easily do something with it if he set his mind to it, but he didn't bother. In fact, he dug a hole in the ground to hide the money and then lazed around.

When the master returned he called his servants together. The first servant happily put ten bags in front of him. 'You gave me five sir, and I have earned five more for you.'

The master was pleased and said, 'Well done, good and faithful servant. You took good care of a few things. Now I will give you many things to care for. Go to my house and celebrate with me.'

The second servant brought in four bags of money. He said happily, 'Lord, you gave me two and I have two more.'

And the master was just as satisfied with him as with the first servant. He said again, 'Well done, good and faithful servant. You took good care of a little. I will give you much. Go in and celebrate with me.'

Then the third servant came. He put the one bag of money in front of his master and said boldly, 'Look, Sir, here is your money. I just put it away in the ground. I knew that you were a very hard man and I was afraid I might lose some of the money and be punished. Now you can have it all back again. I hope you are satisfied that I do not owe you anything.'

But the master was not satisfied at all. He told him, 'You lazy rascal. You knew that I was strict yet still you did nothing about it?' Then turning to one of the other servants, said, 'Take the money away from him and give it to the servant who already has ten bags. He has worked hard and deserves more, but this man has earned nothing at all.'

Jesus explained that one day he would go away to be with his Father in heaven but that he would come back again. When he does he will ask those who say that they are his servants, 'What have you done for me?'

It may not be about what we have done with our money but in what way we have helped our neighbours. Whatever we do for others in his name, it is as if we are doing it for him.

Bible books by Category

OLD TESTAMENT

Pentateuch:
Genesis; Exodus
Leviticus; Numbers
Deuteronomy

History:
Joshua; Judges; Ruth
1 Samuel; 2 Samuel
1 Kings; 2 Kings
1 Chronicles
2 Chronicles
Ezra; Nehemiah
Esther

Poetry:
Job; Psalms
Proverbs
Ecclesiastes
Song of Songs

Major Prophets:
Isaiah; Jeremiah
Lamentations; Ezekiel
Daniel

Minor Prophets:
Hosea; Joel
Amos; Obadiah
Jonah; Micah
Nahum; Habakkuk
Zephaniah
Haggai; Zechariah
Malachi

How many days
did God take to
create the world?
Page 8-9

What did
the princess
find by the
river?
Page 65

What did Mary do
with her expensive
jar of perfume?
Page 229

On what day did
God create
flowers? Page 8

How did Moses help
some girls at a well?
Page 69

What did the disciples
and Jesus eat at the
Last Supper?
Page 233

Bible books by Category

Who washed the
disciples' feet?
Page 232

NEW TESTAMENT

History:
Matthew; Mark
Luke; John; Acts

Paul's Epistles:
Romans
1 Corinthians
2 Corinthians
Galatians
Ephesians
Philippians
Colossians
1 Thessalonians
2 Thessalonians
1 Timothy
2 Timothy
Titus; Philemon

General Epistles:
Hebrews; James
1 Peter
2 Peter
1 John
2 John
3 John
Jude

Revelation

Who sent out a dove
to find out about a
flood?
Page 19

What did Jesus change
water into?
Page 196

Who made a pot of
soup for his brother?
Page 38

What did God make
on day six of
creation?
Page 9

Virtues, Values and Truth

Virtues and Values

Truth about God

On page 83
See how God gave
his people water.

On page 109-113 you will see
how God's word is true.

Find out on page 207 how
Jesus fed thousands of
people.

On page 275 read about some girls
who forgot their lamps.

Key Characters

Who said that he wasn't worthy to untie the straps on Jesus' sandals?
Page 193

What God tells us to do

God tells us that his word is true and we must believe in his son Jesus Christ if we are to be saved. It is important therefore to read God's word and to pray to God for understanding.

The stories in this collection are a good introduction to what God says in his word. If you have enjoyed these and found that God has taught you through them you will find more stories and truths if you begin to read the complete Bible for yourself.

There are many other stories about Samuel and David, the disciples and Paul as well as the Lord Jesus Christ.

In fact, in the Bible, one of the writers has said that, if everything that could be written about Jesus was written, the whole world wouldn't be big enough for all the books.

This book is only the start of a wonderful adventure. Read God's word. Pray for understanding and believe in the Lord Jesus Christ, for the salvation of your soul and the forgiveness of your sins.

CHRISTIAN FOCUS PUBLICATIONS

Christian Focus | Christian Heritage | CF4K | Mentor

Christian Focus Publications publishes books for adults and children under its four main imprints: Christian Focus, CF4K, Mentor and Christian Heritage. Our books reflect our conviction that God's Word is reliable and Jesus is the way to know him, and live for ever with him.

Our children's publication list includes a Sunday School curriculum that covers pre-school to early teens, and puzzle and activity books. We also publish personal and family devotional titles, biographies and inspirational stories that children will love.

If you are looking for quality Bible teaching for children then we have an excellent range of Bible stories and age-specific theological books.

From pre-school board books to teenage apologetics, we have it covered!

Find us at our web page:
www.christianfocus.com

CF4•K
Because you're never
too young to know Jesus